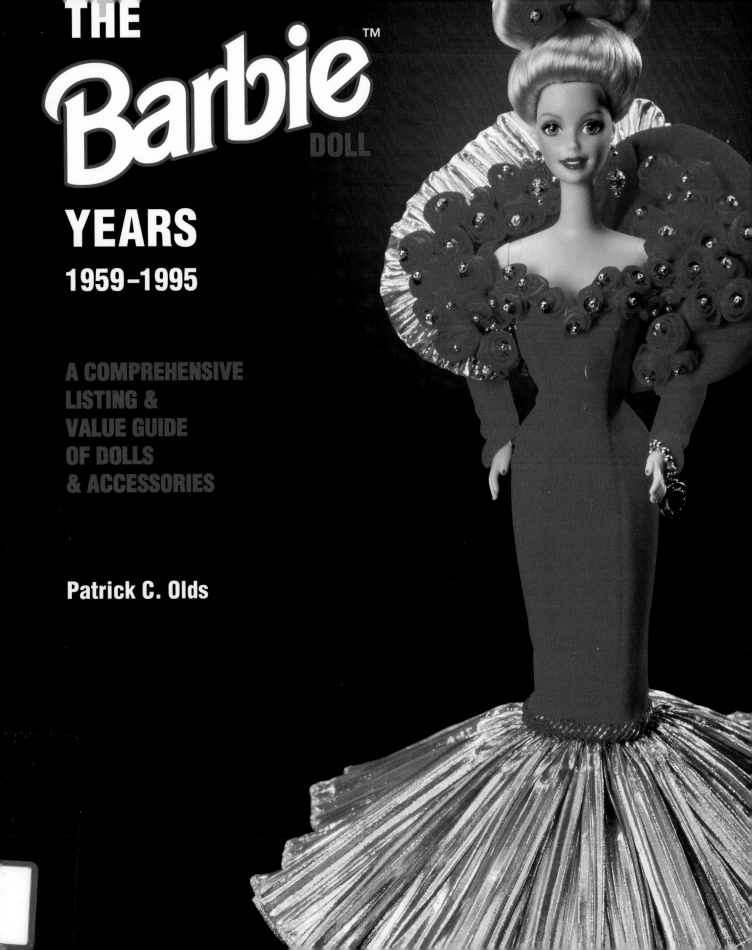

THE *Barbie* DOLL ™

YEARS

1959–1995

**A COMPREHENSIVE
LISTING &
VALUE GUIDE
OF DOLLS
& ACCESSORIES**

Patrick C. Olds

THE

Barbie™ DOLL

YEARS
1959–1995

**A COMPREHENSIVE
LISTING &
VALUE GUIDE
OF DOLLS
& ACCESSORIES**

Patrick C. Olds

COLLECTOR BOOKS
A Division of Schroeder Publishing Co., Inc.

On the cover:

To celebrate Mattel's 50th anniversary, this porcelain Barbie doll was issued in a limited edition of 23,000. This doll is embellished with 50 fabric red roses. Her bracelet has a charm with the Mattel logo on it. The doll was designed by Mattel's Carol Spencer, who also designed the Gold Jubilee doll in 1994.

Searching For A Publisher?

We are always looking for knowledgeable people considered to be experts within their fields. If you feel that there is a real need for a book on your collectible subject and have a large comprehensive collection contact Collector Books.

Additional copies of this book may be ordered from:

COLLECTOR BOOKS
P.O. Box 3009
Paducah, Kentucky 42002-3009
or
Patrick C. Olds
P.O. Box 293322
Nashville, Tennessee 37229-3322

$16.95. Add $2.00 for postage and handling.

Copyright: Patrick C. Olds, 1996

Printed in the USA

Printed by IMAGE GRAPHICS, INC., Paducah, Kentucky

CONTENTS

INTRODUCTION

When my wife began collecting Barbie dolls I realized the need for a reference which contained detailed information such as production years and item numbers. Much research had been done to come up with the most extensive list of Barbie and family dolls and products which have been manufactured in the last 36 years. I hope that you, the collector, will be pleased with my work and that this text will be of benefit now and for years to come.

This text is unique in the fact that it is referenced in different ways: alphabetically, numerically (stock number), doll type, and year of issue, and it includes miscellaneous listings. Therefore, this text should be an invaluable asset to the collector, who might need further information about a particular doll or Barbie product.

PRICE INFORMATION

The current values in this book should be used as a guide only, these prices were gathered from shows, mailing lists, dealers, Barbie clubs, auctions, and from various other sources. Prices vary from different parts of the country. The condition of the doll and/or box plays an important part in the determination of the value of the doll. All prices listed here are based on NRFB condition.

Although every attempt has been made, it is impossible to determine values for every item listed in this book. All values are current as of 1995. Further revisions of this book will list values of items not given a value at this time. Every effort is being made to have prices listed for all items marked with N/A or RTL for the next edition.

ACKNOWLEDGMENTS

I dedicate this book to you, the avid Barbie doll collector, and my wife, Zona, another avid Barbie doll collector.

I would like to especially thank my wife for spending all our money on Barbie dolls so that I had to write this book. It has been a great experience and a very time-consuming one. She even acted as photographer for some of the pictures in this book and wrote their captions.

Karl Olsen, of Toys 'R' Us in Goodlettsville, TN, for all his help in providing information.

All of the dealers and collectors who have given of their time to help with information over the past several months. Special appreciation goes to:

Kitty's Collectibles
6568 Modoc Lane
Evergreen, CO 80439
(303) 670-9312

Mid–Tenn Collectibles
217 Main Street
Goodlettsville, TN 37072
(615) 851-0725
Always buying Mackies and other high-end Barbie Dolls. Will buy entire collections.

Sharon's Doll Paradise
401 Marty Drive
Bowling Green, KY 42101
(502) 782-0033
Buy • Sell • Trade

Note: The author is scheduled to appear at several 1996 shows sponsored by Kitty's Collectibles. The dates and cities are listed below. Contact Kitty for more details.

Cincinnati, OH..........March 17   Minneapolis, MN ....July 28
Raleigh, NC..................April 28   Detroit, MI ....August 11
Houston, TX ....June 23

THE BARBIE FAMILY

The Barbie doll family is broken down into three sections. Barbie doll's family, friends, and pets.

BARBIE b. 1959

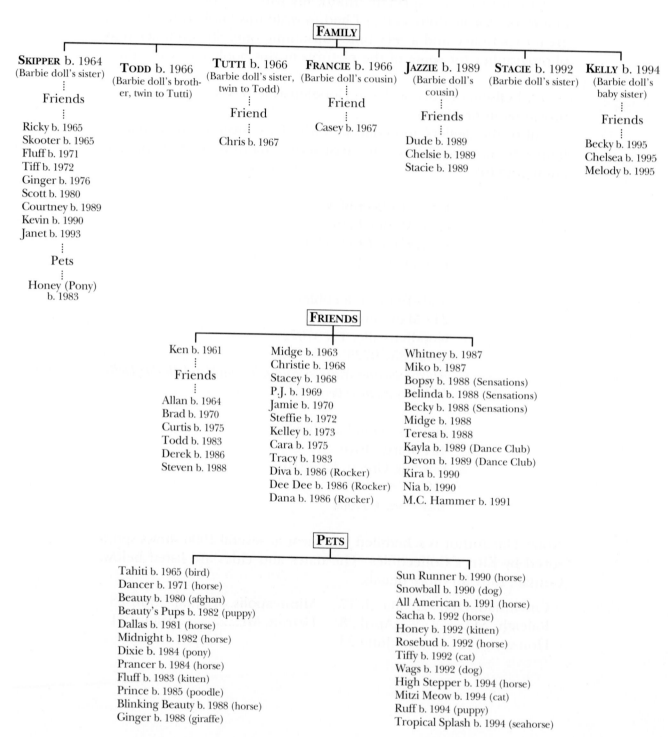

FAMILY

SKIPPER b. 1964
(Barbie doll's sister)
⋮
Friends
⋮
Ricky b. 1965
Skooter b. 1965
Fluff b. 1971
Tiff b. 1972
Ginger b. 1976
Scott b. 1980
Courtney b. 1989
Kevin b. 1990
Janet b. 1993

Pets
⋮
Honey (Pony)
b. 1983

TODD b. 1966
(Barbie doll's brother, twin to Tutti)

TUTTI b. 1966
(Barbie doll's sister, twin to Todd)
⋮
Friend
⋮
Chris b. 1967

FRANCIE b. 1966
(Barbie doll's cousin)
⋮
Friend
⋮
Casey b. 1967

JAZZIE b. 1989
(Barbie doll's cousin)
⋮
Friends
⋮
Dude b. 1989
Chelsie b. 1989
Stacie b. 1989

STACIE b. 1992
(Barbie doll's sister)

KELLY b. 1994
(Barbie doll's baby sister)
⋮
Friends
⋮
Becky b. 1995
Chelsea b. 1995
Melody b. 1995

FRIENDS

Ken b. 1961
⋮
Friends
⋮
Allan b. 1964
Brad b. 1970
Curtis b. 1975
Todd b. 1983
Derek b. 1986
Steven b. 1988

Midge b. 1963
Christie b. 1968
Stacey b. 1968
P.J. b. 1969
Jamie b. 1970
Steffie b. 1972
Kelley b. 1973
Cara b. 1975
Tracy b. 1983
Diva b. 1986 (Rocker)
Dee Dee b. 1986 (Rocker)
Dana b. 1986 (Rocker)

Whitney b. 1987
Miko b. 1987
Bopsy b. 1988 (Sensations)
Belinda b. 1988 (Sensations)
Becky b. 1988 (Sensations)
Midge b. 1988
Teresa b. 1988
Kayla b. 1989 (Dance Club)
Devon b. 1989 (Dance Club)
Kira b. 1990
Nia b. 1990
M.C. Hammer b. 1991

PETS

Tahiti b. 1965 (bird)
Dancer b. 1971 (horse)
Beauty b. 1980 (afghan)
Beauty's Pups b. 1982 (puppy)
Dallas b. 1981 (horse)
Midnight b. 1982 (horse)
Dixie b. 1984 (pony)
Prancer b. 1984 (horse)
Fluff b. 1983 (kitten)
Prince b. 1985 (poodle)
Blinking Beauty b. 1988 (horse)
Ginger b. 1988 (giraffe)

Sun Runner b. 1990 (horse)
Snowball b. 1990 (dog)
All American b. 1991 (horse)
Sacha b. 1992 (horse)
Honey b. 1992 (kitten)
Rosebud b. 1992 (horse)
Tiffy b. 1992 (cat)
Wags b. 1992 (dog)
High Stepper b. 1994 (horse)
Mitzi Meow b. 1994 (cat)
Ruff b. 1994 (puppy)
Tropical Splash b. 1994 (seahorse)

ABBREVIATIONS

Here is a list of abbreviations that you will often see used in listings or advertisements.

ACC	Accessories
B.L.	Bendable leg
B.C.	Bubble cut
BK	Book
C	Complete
CLO	Clothes
C/M	Complete & mint
C.T.	Close toe
D.S.S.	Department store special
EC	Excellent condition
FC	Fair condition
FUR	Furniture
GC	Good condition
GS	Gift set
HTF	Hard to find
I	Incomplete
JE	Jewelry
M	Mint
MIB	Mint in box
MIP	Mint in package
MISC	Miscellaneous
MOC	Mint on card
MU	Make-up
NM	Near mint
NRFB	Never removed from box
OF	Outfit
OO	Original outfit
OSS	Original swimsuit
OT	Open toe
OW	Otherwise
PC	Poor condition
PD	Paper doll
RE	Real estate
REC	Record
RTL	Retail
SD	Store display
S.L.	Straight leg
SS	Swimsuit
TNT	Twist & turn
VEH	Vehicles
VGC	Very good condition
2XRTL	Twice retail price

BARBIE® DOLLS

Listed Alphabetically

DOLL	NUMBER	YEAR	VALUE	STORE/COLLECTION
#1 Ponytail (blonde)	850	1959	$4200.00	
#1 Ponytail (brunette)	850	1959	$4600.00	
#2 Ponytail (blonde)	850	1959	$4000.00	
#2 Ponytail (brunette)	850	1959	$5100.00	
#3 Ponytail (blonde)	850	1960	$800.00	
#3 Ponytail (brunette)	850	1960	$798.00	
#4 Ponytail (blonde)	850	1960	$695.00	
#4 Ponytail (brunette)	850	1960	$250.00	
#5 Ponytail (brunette with arm tag)	850	1961	$412.00	
#5 Ponytail (lemon blonde with arm tag)	850	1961	$240.00	
#5 Ponytail (pale blonde with arm tag)	850	1961	$420.00	
#5 Ponytail (redhead with arm tag)	850	1961	$450.00	
#6 Bubble Cut (bright Titian)	850	1961	$850.00	
#6 Ponytail (ash blonde)	850	1962	$185.00	
#6 Ponytail (blonde)	850	1962	$245.00	
#6 Ponytail (brunette)	850	1962	$235.00	
#6 Ponytail (redhead)	850	1962	$195.00	
#6 Wheat Blonde	850	1962	$265.00	
#6 Yellow Blonde	850	1962	$195.00	
#7 Ponytail	850	1962	$150.00	
25th Anniversary	3939	1972	$600.00	Montgomery Wards
35th Anniversary Curly Bangs (blonde)	N/A	1994	$525.00	Mattel's Barbie Festival
35th Anniversary Curly Bangs (redhead)	N/A	1994	$525.00	Mattel's Barbie Festival
35th Anniversary Nostalgic (blonde)	11589	1994	$25.00	
35th Anniversary Nostalgic (brunette)	11782	1994	$45.00	
Action Accents Set (auburn)	1585	1969	$900.00	Sears
Air Force	3360	1991	$50.00	Stars 'n Stripes
Air Force (Thunderbirds)	11552	1994	$75.00	
All American	9423	1991	$20.00	
American Beauty Queen	3137	1991	$20.00	
American Beauty Queen (black)	3245	1991	$25.00	
American Girl (Bend. Leg, Color Magic Face)	1070	1966	$1350.00	
American Girl (Bendable Leg)	1070	1965	$800.00	
American Girl (Bendable Leg)	1070	1966	$1125.00	
American Girl (Bendable Leg, Side Part)	1070	1965	$3300.00	
American Girl (blonde)	1070	1965	$1650.00	
American Girl (brown)	1070	1965	$295.00	
American Girl (brunette)	1070	1965	$1195.00	
American Girl (pale blonde)	1070	1965	$750.00	
American Girl (redhead)	1070	1965	$325.00	

BARBIE® DOLLS

Listed Alphabetically

DOLL	NUMBER	YEAR	VALUE	STORE/COLLECTION
Angel Face	5640	1983	$50.00	
Angel Lights	10610	1993	$125.00	Christmas
Animal Lovin'	1350	1989	$35.00	
Animal Lovin' (black)	4824	1989	$30.00	
Anniversary Star	2282	1992	$40.00	Wal-Mart
Army	3936	1989	$35.00	American Beauty Collection
Army Desert Storm	1234	1993	$25.00	Stars 'n Stripes
Army Desert Storm (black)	N/A	1993	$25.00	Stars 'n Stripes
Army (Dress Blues)	3966	1990	$35.00	Stars 'n Stripes
Astronaut	2449	1986	$95.00	
Astronaut	12149	1994	$35.00	Toys 'R' Us
Astronaut (black)	1207	1986	$80.00	
Astronaut (black)	12150	1994	$45.00	Toys 'R' Us
Australian	7344	1993	$22.00	Dolls of the World Series
Back to School	N/A	1992	$25.00	Supermarket
Ballerina	9093	1979	$50.00	
Ballerina	9093	1980	$50.00	
Ballerina	4983	1983	$75.00	Mervyn's
Ballerina (1st issue)	9093	1976	$25.00	
Ballerina (2nd issue)	9093	1976	$25.00	
Ballerina on Tour	9093	1976	$175.00	Department Store
Ballerina on Tour (reissue)	9093	1978	$60.00	
Ballroom Beauty	3678	1991	$30.00	Wal-Mart
Barbie and the All Stars	9099	1990	$25.00	
Barbie and the Beats	2751	1990	$25.00	
Barbie and the Sensations Set	5509	1988	N/A	
Barbie Doll	1070	1967	N/A	
Barbie Doll	N/A	1990	$45.00	Children's Palace
Barbie Doll	1511	1991	$300.00	McGlynns Bakery
Barbie Doll (auburn)	N/A	1966	N/A	
Barbie Doll (black)	1293	1980	$95.00	
Barbie Doll (black)	N/A	1990	$45.00	Children's Palace
Barbie Doll (black)	1534	1991	$250.00	McGlynns Bakery
Barbie Doll (blonde)	N/A	1966	N/A	
Barbie Doll (brunette)	N/A	1966	N/A	
Barbie Doll (brunette)	1190	1969	N/A	
Barbie Doll (new swimsuit)	1190	1970	$365.00	
Barbie Doll (Side Part)	N/A	1965	N/A	
Barbie Doll (standard)	1190	1967	$350.00	
Barbie for President	3722	1991	$50.00	Toys 'R' Us

BARBIE® DOLLS

Listed Alphabetically

DOLL	NUMBER	YEAR	VALUE	STORE/COLLECTION
Barbie For President (black)	3940	1991	$50.00	Toys 'R' Us
Barbie & Friends	4431	1983	$40.00	
Barbie & Ken Thunderbirds (Air Force)	11581	1993	$40.00	Stars 'n Stripes
Barbie & Snowball Her Pet Dog	7272	1990	$18.00	
Barbie Style	5315	1990	$45.00	Applause
Baseball	N/A	1993	$40.00	Target
Bath Blast	4159	1993	$10.00	
Bath Blast (black)	3830	1993	$10.00	
Bath Magic	5274	1992	$15.00	
Bath Magic (black)	7951	1992	$12.00	
Bathtime Fun	9601	1991	$12.00	
Bathtime Fun (black)	9603	1991	$12.00	
Baywatch	13199	1995	$20.00	
Baywatch (black)	13258	1995	$20.00	
Beach Blast	3237	1989	$10.00	
Beach Time	9102	1984	$25.00	
Beautiful Blues Set (brunette)	3303	1967	N/A	Sears
Beautiful Bride	9599	1976	$300.00	Department Store
Beautiful Bride	9599	1976	$75.00	
Beautiful Bride	9907	1978	$200.00	
Beauty Belle	4553	1991	$25.00	Applause
Beauty Secrets	1290	1980	$300.00	Barbie Convention
Beauty Secrets	1290	1980	$45.00	
Bedtime	11079	1994	$15.00	
Bedtime (black)	11184	1994	$15.00	
Bendable Leg (American Girl style)	1070	1965	$500.00	
Bendable Leg (Bubble Cut)	1070	1965	$1300.00	
Bendable Leg (Side Part Flip)	1070	1965	$2995.00	
Benefit Ball	1521	1992	$150.00	Classique Collection
Benefit Performance	5475	1988	$300.00	Porcelain
Benetton	9404	1992	$35.00	
Benneton Shopping	4873	1991	$25.00	
Bicyclin'	11689	1994	$30.00	
Bicyclin' (black)	11817	1994	$25.00	
Birthday	11333	1994	$25.00	
Birthday	12954	1995	$20.00	
Birthday (black)	11334	1994	$25.00	
Birthday (black)	12955	1995	$25.00	
Birthday (Hispanic)	13253	1995	$25.00	
Birthday Party	3388	1993	$30.00	

BARBIE® DOLLS

Listed Alphabetically

DOLL	NUMBER	YEAR	VALUE	STORE/COLLECTION
Birthday Party (black)	7948	1993	$30.00	
Birthday Surprise	3679	1992	$35.00	
Birthday Surprise (black)	4051	1992	$20.00	
Bloomingdale's Donna Karan NY (blonde)	14545	1995	$95.00	Bloomingdale's
Bloomingdale's Donna Karan NY (brunette)	14452	1995	$110.00	Bloomingdale's
Blossom Beauty	3412	1991	$45.00	Shopco/Venture
Blossom Beauty	3817	1992	$280.00	Sears
Blue Elegance	1879	1992	$30.00	Hill's
Blue Rhapsody	1708	1986	$900.00	Porcelain
Blue Rhapsody	1364	1991	$275.00	Service Merchandise
BMine	N/A	1993	$20.00	Supermarket
Brazilian	9094	1990	$35.00	Dolls of the World Series
Bridesmaid	9608	1991	$30.00	
Bubble Angel	12443	1995	$12.00	
Bubble Angel (black)	12444	1995	$12.00	
Bubble Cut (blonde)	850	1961	$225.00	
Bubble Cut (blonde)	850	1962	$200.00	
Bubble Cut (bright Titian)	850	1962	N/A	
Bubble Cut (brown)	850	1962	$200.00	
Bubble Cut (brownette)	850	1961	$750.00	
Bubble Cut (brunette)	850	1962	$200.00	
Bubble Cut (redhead)	850	1961	$225.00	
Bubble Cut (redhead)	850	1962	$200.00	
Busy Barbie	3311	1972	$150.00	
Busy Gal (brunette with curly bangs)	N/A	1995	$50.00	
Butterfly Princess	13051	1995	$22.00	
Butterfly Princess (black)	13052	1995	$22.00	
Butterfly Princess (Hispanic)	13238	1995	$22.00	
Caboodles	3157	1993	$20.00	
California Dream	4439	1988	$25.00	
Camp	11074	1994	$12.00	
Canadian	4928	1988	$75.00	Dolls of the World Series
Case with Doll (Swirl Ponytail)	2000	1966	$1000.00	
Chinese	11180	1993	$24.00	Dolls of the World Series
Christian Dior No. 1	13168	1995	$175.00	Designer Collection
Circus Star	13257	1995	$90.00	F.A.O. Schwarz
City Sophisticate	12005	1994	$95.00	Service Merchandise
City Style	10149	1993	$95.00	Classique Collection
Colonial	12578	1995	$25.00	American Stories Series
Color Magic (black turns red)	1150	1965	$1850.00	

BARBIE® DOLLS

Listed Alphabetically

DOLL	NUMBER	YEAR	VALUE	STORE/COLLECTION
Color Magic (cardboard box, blonde)	1150	1966	$1400.00	
Color Magic (cardboard box, midnight black)	1150	1966	$1850.00	
Color Magic (plastic box, blonde)	1150	1966	$1100.00	
Color Magic (plastic box, midnight black)	1150	1966	$1500.00	
Cool Looks	5947	1990	$25.00	Toys 'R' Us
Cool 'n Sassy	1490	1992	$25.00	Toys 'R' Us
Cool 'n Sassy (black)	4110	1992	$25.00	Toys 'R' Us
Cool Times	3022	1989	$25.00	
Costume Ball	7123	1991	$25.00	
Costume Ball (black)	7134	1991	$25.00	
Country Bride	13614	1995	$12.00	Wal-Mart
Country Looks	N/A	1992	$25.00	Ames
Country & Western Star	12097	1994	$30.00	Wal-Mart
Country & Western Star (black)	N/A	1994	$30.00	Wal-Mart
Country & Western Star (Hispanic)	N/A	1994	$30.00	Wal-Mart
Crystal	4598	1984	$35.00	
Crystal (black)	4859	1984	$40.00	
Crystal Rhapsody	N/A	1992	$450.00	Porcelain
Crystal Rhapsody (brunette)	10201	1992	$750.00	Disney
Cute 'n Cool	2954	1991	$40.00	Target
Cut 'n Style #1 (blonde)	12639	1994	$12.00	
Cut 'n Style #2 (black)	12642	1994	$12.00	
Cut 'n Style (brunette)	12643	1994	$12.00	
Cut 'n Style (redhead)	12644	1994	$12.00	
Czechoslovakian	7330	1991	$110.00	Dolls of the World Series
Dance Club	3509	1989	$30.00	
Dance Magic	4836	1990	$25.00	
Dance Magic (black)	7080	1990	$20.00	
Dance Moves	13083	1995	$15.00	
Dance Moves (black)	13086	1995	$15.00	
Dance 'n Twirl	11902	1994	$55.00	
Dance 'n Twirl (black)	12143	1994	$50.00	
Day-To-Night	7929	1985	$35.00	
Day-To-Night (black)	7945	1985	$25.00	
Day-To-Night (Hispanic)	7944	1985	$30.00	
Dayton Hudson Cute 'n Cool	2954	1991	$25.00	
Dazzlin' Date	N/A	1992	$40.00	Target
Deluxe Quick Curl (Jergens)	9217	1976	$60.00	
Deluxe Tropical	2996	1985	$45.00	
Denim 'n Lace	2452	1992	$35.00	Ames

Barbie® Dolls

Listed Alphabetically

Doll	Number	Year	Value	Store/Collection
Disney Character Barbie	9835	1990	$50.00	Disney
Disney Fun	10247	1992	$45.00	Disney
Disney Special (with mouse hat)	4385	1991	$50.00	Children's Palace
Dolls of the World Set	13939	1995	$75.00	Dolls of the World Series
Dorothy (Wizard of Oz)	12701	1995	$50.00	Hollywood Legends
Dr. Barbie	3850	1988	$50.00	
Dr. Barbie (black with white baby)	11814	1994	$50.00	Toys 'R' Us
Dr. Barbie (brunette)	11160	1994	$250.00	Mattel Festival Doll
Dr. Barbie (white with black baby)	11160	1994	$50.00	Toys 'R' Us
Dr. Barbie (with 3 babies)	14309	1995	$20.00	
Dramatic New Living Barbie	1585	1971	$65.00	
Dream Bride Spec. Wedding Gown	1623	1991	$30.00	Barbie Wedding Dreams
Dream Dancing	11902	1994	Rtl	
Dream Dancing (black)	12143	1994	Rtl	
Dream Date	5868	1983	$45.00	
Dream Fantasy	7335	1990	$50.00	Wal-Mart
Dream Glow	2248	1986	$45.00	
Dream Glow (black)	2242	1986	$40.00	
Dream Glow (Hispanic)	1647	1985	$70.00	
Dream Princess	N/A	1992	$45.00	Sears
Dream Time	9180	1985	$40.00	Toys 'R' Us
Dream Wedding	N/A	1993	$45.00	Toys 'R' Us
Dream Wedding (black)	10713	1993	$45.00	Toys 'R' Us
Dress Me	5696	1991	$250.00	Barbie Loves a Fairytale
Dress 'n Fun	10776	1994	$6.00	
Dress 'n Fun (black)	12143	1994	$6.00	
Dress 'n Fun (Hispanic)	11102	1994	$6.00	
Dutch	11104	1994	$24.00	Dolls of the World Series
Earring Magic (black)	2374	1993	$20.00	
Earring Magic (blonde)	7014	1993	$20.00	
Earring Magic (brunette)	10255	1993	$20.00	
Easter Fun	11276	1993	$45.00	Supermarket
Egyptian Queen	11397	1994	$100.00	Great Eras Collection
Elizabethan Queen	12792	1995	$50.00	Great Eras Collection
Emerald Elegance	12322	1994	$40.00	Toys 'R' Us
Emerald Elegance (black)	12323	1994	$30.00	Toys 'R' Us
Empress Bride	4247	1992	$895.00	Bob Mackie
Enchanted Evening	3415	1987	$475.00	Porcelain
Enchanted Evening	37028	1987	$550.00	
Enchanted Evening	2702	1991	$45.00	J.C. Penney

BARBIE® DOLLS

Listed Alphabetically

DOLL	NUMBER	YEAR	VALUE	STORE/COLLECTION
Gift Giving	1922	1986	$20.00	
Gift Giving	1205	1989	$20.00	
Glitter Beach	3602	1993	$25.00	
Glitter Hair (black)	11332	1994	$12.00	
Glitter Hair (blonde)	10965	1994	$12.00	
Glitter Hair (burnette)	10966	1994	$12.00	
Glitter Hair (redhead)	10968	1994	$12.00	
Goddess of the Sun	14056	1995	$225.00	Bob Mackie
Gold	5405	1990	$900.00	Bob Mackie
Gold and Lace	7476	1989	$45.00	Target
Gold Jubilee	12009	1994	$1400.00	Jubilee Series
Gold Medal Olympic Sports	7233	1975	$75.00	
Gold Medal Skater	7262	1975	$75.00	
Gold Medal Skater	7264	1976	$75.00	
Gold Medal Skier	7264	1975	$75.00	
Gold Medal Skier	7262	1976	$125.00	
Gold Medal U. S. Olympics	7233	1976	$75.00	
Gold Medal Winter Sports	9042	1975	$50.00	
Gold Sensation	10246	1993	$450.00	Porcelain
Golden Dreams (1st issue)	1874	1981	$60.00	
Golden Dreams (2nd issue)	3533	1981	$60.00	Department Store
Golden Evening	2587	1991	$40.00	Target
Golden Greetings	7734	1989	$225.00	F.A.O. Schwarz
Golden Winter	10684	1993	$95.00	J.C. Penney
Golf Date	10202	1993	$25.00	Target
Great Shapes	7025	1984	$30.00	
Great Shapes (black)	7834	1984	$25.00	
Great Shapes & Walkman®	7025	1983	$30.00	
Greek	2997	1986	$85.00	Dolls of the World Series
Growin' Pretty Hair	1144	1971	$233.00	
Growin' Pretty Hair	1144	1972	$235.00	Sears
Gymnast	12127	1994	$14.00	
Gymnast (black)	12153	1994	$14.00	
Gymnast (brunette)	11921	1994	$250.00	Mattel Festival Doll
Hair Fair	4043	1967	$90.00	
Hair Fair	4094	1967	$90.00	
Hair Fair (blonde)	4044	1971	$175.00	
Hair's Happening (auburn)	1174	1971	$895.00	
Happy Birthday	1922	1981	$75.00	
Happy Birthday	7913	1991	$40.00	

BARBIE® DOLLS

Listed Alphabetically

DOLL	NUMBER	YEAR	VALUE	STORE/COLLECTION
Happy Birthday (2nd issue)	1922	1983	$25.00	
Happy Birthday (3rd issue)	1922	1984	$20.00	
Happy Birthday (black)	9561	1991	$30.00	
Happy Holidays	1703	1988	$725.00	Happy Holidays Collection
Happy Holidays	3523	1989	$275.00	Happy Holidays Collection
Happy Holidays	4098	1990	$150.00	Happy Holidays Collection
Happy Holidays	1871	1991	$175.00	Happy Holidays Collection
Happy Holidays	1429	1992	$120.00	Happy Holidays Collection
Happy Holidays	10824	1993	$135.00	Happy Holidays Collection
Happy Holidays	12155	1994	$175.00	Happy Holidays Collection
Happy Holidays	12155	1994	$650.00	Mattel Festival Doll
Happy Holidays	14123	1995	$29.00	Happy Holidays Collection
Happy Holidays (black)	4543	1990	$95.00	Happy Holidays Collection
Happy Holidays (black)	2696	1991	$125.00	Happy Holidays Collection
Happy Holidays (black)	2396	1992	$100.00	Happy Holidays Collection
Happy Holidays (black)	10911	1993	$120.00	Happy Holidays Collection
Happy Holidays (black)	12196	1994	$125.00	Happy Holidays Collection
Happy Holidays (black)	14124	1995	$29.00	Happy Holidays Collection
Hawaiian	7470	1975	$50.00	Department Store
Hawaiian #1 (one-piece swimsuit)	7470	1981	$40.00	Department Store
Hawaiian #2 (two-piece swimsuit)	7470	1983	$40.00	Department Store
Hawaiian Fun	5940	1991	$30.00	
Hawaiian Superstar	2289	1978	$400.00	
Hispanic	1292	1980	$95.00	
Holiday Doll	3406	1991	$45.00	Applause
Holiday Dreams	12192	1994	$35.00	Supermarket
Holiday Hostess	10280	1992	$45.00	Supermarket
Holiday Jewel	14311	1995	$190.00	Holiday Porcelain Series
Holiday Memories	14106	1995	$50.00	Hallmark
Hollywood Hair	2308	1993	$35.00	
Home Pretty	2249	1990	$25.00	
Horse Lovin'	1757	1983	$45.00	
Hot Dancin' Set	4841	1990	N/A	
Hot Looks	5756	1991	$35.00	Ames
Hot Skatin'	13511	1995	Rtl	
Hot Skatin' (black)	13512	1995	Rtl	
Ice Capades	7365	1990	$45.00	
Ice Capades (reissue)	9847	1991	$40.00	
Ice Capades (black)	7348	1990	$35.00	
Icelandic	3189	1987	$70.00	Dolls of the World Series

BARBIE® DOLLS

Listed Alphabetically

Doll	Number	Year	Value	Store/Collection
India	3897	1983	$150.00	Dolls of the World Series
Irish	7517	1984	$135.00	Dolls of the World Series
Irish	12998	1995	$24.00	Dolls of the World Series
Island Fun	4061	1988	$25.00	
Italian	1602	1981	$180.00	Dolls of the World Series
Italian	2256	1993	$35.00	Dolls of the World Series
Jamaican	4647	1992	$35.00	Dolls of the World Series
Japanese	9481	1985	$95.00	Dolls of the World Series
Japanese International	9481	1985	$300.00	Barbie Around the World
Jewel Jubilee	2366	1991	$95.00	Sam's Wholesale Club
Jewel Secrets	1737	1987	$35.00	
Jewel Secrets (black)	1756	1987	$25.00	
Jeweled Splendor	14061	1995	$400.00	F.A.O. Schwarz
Kenyan	11181	1994	$25.00	Dolls of the World Series
Kissing (bangs style)	2597	1980	$50.00	
Kissing (extra dress)	2597	1980	$45.00	Department Store
Kissing (parted hair style)	2597	1980	$45.00	
Korean	4929	1988	$85.00	Dolls of the World Series
Lavender Looks	3963	1989	$55.00	Wal-Mart
Lavender Surprise	9049	1989	$45.00	Sears
Lavender Surprise (black)	9588	1989	$50.00	Sears
Lights 'n Lace	9725	1991	$25.00	
Lilac and Lovely	7669	1987	$55.00	Sears
Limited Edition Sale	N/A	1994	$395.00	Mattel Festival Doll
Little Debbie	10123	1994	$75.00	Little Debbie Snack Cakes
Live Action On Stage	1152	1971	$233.00	
Live Action (plastic bag)	1155	1973	$165.00	
Live Action (ranch)	10412	1971	$150.00	Montgomery Wards
Live Action (silver blonde)	1155	1971	$115.00	
Living	1116	1970	$175.00	
Locket Surprise	10963	1994	$14.00	
Locket Surprise (black)	11224	1994	$14.00	
Love to Read	10507	1993	$30.00	Toys 'R' Us
Loving You	7072	1984	$25.00	
Loving You in Red Silver Sensation	7072	1984	$450.00	Barbie Loves New York
Ma-Ba	N/A	1987	$65.00	Campus Collection
Madison Avenue	1539	1991	$200.00	F.A.O. Schwarz
Magic Curl	3856	1982	$30.00	
Magic Curl (black)	3989	1982	$30.00	
Magic Moves	2126	1986	$15.00	

BARBIE® DOLLS

Listed Alphabetically

DOLL	NUMBER	YEAR	VALUE	STORE/COLLECTION
Magic Moves (black)	2127	1986	$35.00	
Malaysian	7329	1991	$35.00	Dolls of the World Series
Malibu (Baggie)	N/A	1976	$20.00	
Malibu Barbie	1067	1975	$45.00	
Malibu Fashion Combo	2753	1978	$50.00	
Malt Shop	4581	1993	$25.00	Toys 'R' Us
Mardi Gras	4930	1990	$100.00	American Beauty Collection
Maria (Sound of Music)	13676	1995	$50.00	Hollywood Legends
Marine	7549	1992	$25.00	Stars 'n Stripes
Marine (black)	7594	1992	$25.00	Stars 'n Stripes
Marine Corps Ken & Barbie Set	4704	1991	$75.00	Stars 'n Stripes
Masquerade Ball	10803	1993	$350.00	Bob Mackie
Mattel 50th Anniversary Porcelain	14479	1995	$700.00	Mattel Anniversary Doll
Mattel Special Curley Bangs (brunette)	N/A	1994	$350.00	Mattel Festival Doll
Medieval Lady	12791	1995	$50.00	Great Eras Collection
Mermaid	1434	1992	$15.00	
Mexican	1917	1989	$75.00	Dolls of the World Series
Midnight Gala	12999	1995	$60.00	Classique Collection
Miss Barbie (Bendable Leg)	1060	1964	N/A	
Miss Barbie (Sleep Eye)	1060	1964	$1500.00	
Miss Barbie with 3 wigs and swing	3704	1964	N/A	Sears
Montgomery Wards Anniversary Doll	3210	1972	$425.00	Montgomery Wards
Moonlight Magic (ethnic)	N/A	1993	$50.00	Toys 'R' Us
Moonlight Rose	3549	1991	$40.00	Hill's
Music Lovin' Barbie	9988	1985	$55.00	
My First Ballerina	1788	1987	$20.00	
My First Ballerina (black)	1801	1987	$25.00	
My First Ballerina dressed as cowgirl	1280	1990	$300.00	Deep in the Heart of Texas
My First Ballerina (Hispanic)	5979	1988	$15.00	
My First Barbie	1281	1988	$15.00	
My First Barbie	1875	1981	$20.00	
My First Barbie	1875	1984	$20.00	
My First Barbie	9942	1990	$10.00	
My First Barbie	3839	1992	$15.00	
My First Barbie	2516	1993	$15.00	
My First Barbie	11294	1994	$10.00	
My First Barbie (2nd issue)	1875	1983	$25.00	
My First Barbie (3rd issue, old style)	9858	1985	$20.00	
My First Barbie (Asian)	11342	1994	$10.00	
My First Barbie (bangs)	1788	1985	$15.00	

Barbie® Dolls

Listed Alphabetically

Doll	Number	Year	Value	Store/Collection
My First Barbie (black)	9858	1985	$15.00	
My First Barbie (black)	1801	1988	$16.00	
My First Barbie (black)	9943	1990	$10.00	
My First Barbie (black)	9943	1991	$10.00	
My First Barbie (black)	3861	1992	$15.00	
My First Barbie (black)	2767	1993	$10.00	
My First Barbie (black)	11340	1994	$10.00	
My First Barbie (black, revised)	1281	1989	$16.00	
My First Barbie Blue Ballet	N/A	1988	$20.00	
My First Barbie (Hispanic)	9944	1991	$20.00	
My First Barbie (Hispanic)	3860	1992	$15.00	
My First Barbie (Hispanic)	2770	1993	$10.00	
My First Barbie (Hispanic)	11341	1994	$10.00	
My First Barbie (Hispanic, revised)	1282	1989	$15.00	
My First Barbie (revised)	1280	1989	$15.00	
My First Hispanic Princess	9943	1990	$25.00	
My First Princess	9943	1990	$25.00	
My First Princess	13064	1995	$10.00	
My First Princess (Asian)	13067	1995	10.00	
My First Princess (black)	13065	1995	$10.00	
My First Princess (Hispanic)	13066	1995	$10.00	
My Size	2517	1992	$175.00	
My Size	2517	1993	$175.00	
My Size	2517	1994	$150.00	
My Size Bride	12052	1994	$175.00	
My Size Bride (black)	12053	1994	$150.00	
My Size Princess Ballerina	13767	1995	$175.00	
My Size Princess Ballerina (black)	13768	1995	$175.00	
Native American #1	1753	1993	$45.00	Dolls of the World Series
Native American #2	11609	1994	$24.00	Dolls of the World Series
Native American #3	12699	1995	$24.00	Dolls of the World Series
Navy	9693	1991	$25.00	Stars 'n Stripes
Navy (black)	9694	1991	$28.00	Stars 'n Stripes
Neptune Fantasy	4248	1992	$950.00	Bob Mackie
Neptune Fantasy face dressed magician	4248	1994	$450.00	Magic of Barbie in Birmingham
New Living (auburn)	1116	1970	$225.00	
New Living (blonde)	1116	1970	$225.00	
New Talking Dinner Dazzle Set (blonde)	1551	1967	N/A	Sears
Newport #1	7807	1974	$200.00	
Newport #2	7807	1974	$200.00	

BARBIE® DOLLS

Listed Alphabetically

DOLL	NUMBER	YEAR	VALUE	STORE/COLLECTION
Newport, The Sports Set (blonde)	7807	1973	$175.00	
Nigerian	7376	1990	$55.00	Dolls of the World Series
Night Dazzle	12191	1994	$65.00	J.C. Penney
Night Dazzle	12191	1994	$650.00	Mattel Festival Doll
Night Sensation	2921	1991	$195.00	F.A.O. Schwarz
North West Barbie Convention Dolls	None	1990	$350.00	Barbie Convention
Nutcracker	5472	1992	$250.00	Ballet Series
Olympic Skating Star	4549	1987	$37.00	
Opening Night	N/A	1993	$95.00	Classique Collection
Oriental	3262	1981	$180.00	Dolls of the World Series
Paint & Dazzle (black)	10058	1993	$20.00	
Paint & Dazzle (blonde)	10039	1993	$20.00	
Paint & Dazzle (brunette)	10059	1993	$20.00	
Paint & Dazzle (redhead)	10057	1993	$20.00	
Parisian	1600	1981	$150.00	Dolls of the World Series
Parisian	9843	1991	$35.00	Dolls of the World Series
Party in Pink	2909	1991	$35.00	Ames
Party Lace	4843	1989	$50.00	Hill's
Party Perfect	1876	1992	$45.00	Shopco/Venture
Party Pink	4629	1987	$10.00	
Party Pink	7637	1989	$15.00	Winn Dixie
Party Premiere	2001	1992	$25.00	Supermarket
Party Pretty	5955	1990	$28.00	Target
Party Sensation	9025	1990	$35.00	Sam's Wholesale Club
Party Time	12243	1994	$23.00	Toys 'R' Us
Party Treats	4885	1990	$20.00	Toys 'R' Us
Peach Blossom	7009	1992	$45.00	Sam's Wholesale Club
Peach Pretty	4870	1989	$50.00	K-Mart
Peaches 'n Cream	7926	1985	$25.00	
Peaches 'n Cream (black)	9516	1985	$20.00	
Peppermint Princess	13598	1995	$60.00	Princess Collection
Pepsi Spirit	4869	1990	$100.00	Toys 'R' Us
Perfume Pretty	4551	1988	$30.00	
Perfume Pretty (black)	4552	1988	$30.00	
Peruvian	2995	1986	$75.00	Dolls of the World Series
Picnic Pretty	3808	1992	$30.00	Osco Drugs
Pilgrim	12577	1995	$23.00	American Stories Series
Pink Jubilee (25th Anniversary Wal-Mart)	4589	1988	$75.00	Wal-Mart
Pink Jubilee	None	1989	$2000.00	30th Anniversary
Pink & Pretty	3554	1982	$40.00	

Barbie® Dolls

Listed Alphabetically

Doll	Number	Year	Value	Store/Collection
Pink & Pretty Modeling Set	5239	1982	$88.00	
Pink Sensation	5410	1990	$25.00	Winn Dixie
Pioneer	12680	1995	$23.00	American Stories Series
Plantation Belle	5351	1992	$750.00	Disney
Plantation Belle	7526	1992	$250.00	Porcelain
Platinum	2704	1991	$750.00	Bob Mackie
Plus 3	N/A	1976	$75.00	Ben Franklin
Pog Barbie	13239	1994	$15.00	Toys 'R' Us
Police Officer	10688	1993	$31.00	Toys 'R' Us
Polly Pockets	12412	1994	$40.00	Hill's
Polynesian	12700	1995	$24.00	Dolls of the World Series
Posable	8414	1965	N/A	Montgomery Wards
Pretty Changes	2598	1980	$35.00	
Pretty Dreams	13611	1995	$20.00	
Pretty Dreams (black)	13630	1995	$20.00	
Pretty Hearts	2901	1991	$30.00	Supermarket
Pretty Hearts	14473	1995	$5.00	
Pretty in Plaid	5413	1992	$25.00	Target
Pretty in Purple	3117	1992	$45.00	K-Mart
Pretty in Purple (black)	3121	1992	45.00	K-Mart
Pretty Surprise	9823	1992	$20.00	
Purple Passion	13555	1995	$30.00	Toys 'R' Us
Purple Passion (black)	13554	1995	$30.00	Toys 'R' Us
Queen of Hearts	12046	1994	$230.00	Bob Mackie
Quick Curl (blonde)	4220	1972	$65.00	
Quick Curl with extra outfit	4220	1973	$65.00	Store Promotion
Radiant in Red	1276	1992	$60.00	Toys 'R' Us
Radiant in Red (Hispanic)	N/A	1992	$45.00	Toys 'R' Us
Rainbow	N/A	1994	$595.00	Mattel Festival Doll
Rappin' Rockin'	3248	1992	$30.00	
Rapunzel	13016	1995	$40.00	Children's Collector Series
Red Romance	3161	1992	$30.00	Supermarket
Red Velvet	N/A	1994	$495.00	Mattel Festival Doll
Regal Reflections	4116	1992	$200.00	Spiegel
Rocker	1140	1986	$30.00	
Rocker Dancin' Action	3055	1987	$30.00	
Rockette	2017	1992	$225.00	F.A.O. Schwarz
Rollerblade	2214	1992	$16.00	
Rollerskating	1880	1981	$50.00	
Romantic Bride	1861	1993	$30.00	

BARBIE® DOLLS

Listed Alphabetically

DOLL	NUMBER	YEAR	VALUE	STORE/COLLECTION
Royal	1981	1981	$180.00	Dolls of the World Series
Royal Invitation	2969	1993	$125.00	Spiegel
Royal Romance	1858	1992	$85.00	Sam's Wholesale Club
Royal Splendor	10950	1993	$375.00	Porcelain
Ruffle Fun	12433	1994	$12.00	
Ruffle Fun (black)	12434	1994	$12.00	
Ruffle Fun (Hispanic)	12435	1994	$12.00	
Russian	1916	1989	$75.00	Dolls of the World Series
Sapphire Dreams	13255	1995	$60.00	Toys 'R' Us
Satin Nights #1 (all white earrings)	1886	1992	$95.00	Service Merchandise
Satin Nights #2 (silver and white earrings)	1886	1992	$95.00	Service Merchandise
Savy Shopper	12152	1994	$175.00	Bloomingdale's
Scarlett Green Velvet (1st in series)	12045	1994	$95.00	Hollywood Legends
Scarlett in BBQ Dress	12997	1995	$85.00	Hollywood Legends
Scarlett in Black & White (New Orleans)	13254	1995	$85.00	Hollywood Legends
Scarlett in Red Dress	12815	1995	$85.00	Hollywood Legends
School Fun	2721	1991	$20.00	Toys 'R' Us
School Spirit	N/A	1992	$20.00	Toys 'R' Us
School Spirit (black)	N/A	1992	$20.00	Toys 'R' Us
Schooltime Fun	13741	1995	$20.00	Supermarket
Scottish	3263	1981	$140.00	Dolls of the World Series
Scottish	9845	1991	$40.00	Dolls of the World Series
Sea Holiday	5471	1992	$25.00	Toys 'R' Us
Sea Pearl Mermaid	13940	1995	$25.00	Hill's
Sears 100th Anniversary Celebration	2998	1985	$75.00	Sears
Season's Greetings	12384	1994	$125.00	Sam's Wholesale Club
Secret Hearts	7902	1993	$20.00	
Secret Hearts (black)	3836	1993	$25.00	
Sensations	4931	1988	$40.00	
Shopping Chic	14009	1995	$65.00	Spiegel
Shopping Fun	10051	1992	$30.00	Meijers
Shopping Spree	12749	1994	$25.00	F.A.O. Schwarz
Silken Flame (blonde)	11099	1993	$750.00	Disney
Silken Flame (brunette)	1249	1994	$225.00	Porcelain
Silver Screen	11652	1993	$150.00	F.A.O. Schwarz
Silver Starlight	11305	1992	$450.00	Porcelain
Silver Sweetheart	12410	1994	$55.00	Sears
Sing & Dance (black)	13938	1995	Rtl	
Singapore Girl 1	N/A	1991	$125.00	Singapore Airlines
Singapore Girl 2	N/A	1991	$125.00	Singapore Airlines

BARBIE® DOLLS

Listed Alphabetically

DOLL	NUMBER	YEAR	VALUE	STORE/COLLECTION
Ski Fun	7511	1991	$30.00	
Slumber Party	12696	1994	$14.00	
Slumber Party (black)	12697	1994	$14.00	
Snap 'n Play	3550	1992	$15.00	
Snap 'n Play (black)	3556	1992	$15.00	
Snow Princess	11875	1994	$135.00	Enchanted Season
Snow Princess (brunette)	12905	1994	$1800.00	Mattel Festival Doll
Solo in the Spotlight	7613	1990	$295.00	Porcelain
Solo in the Spotlight replica (blonde)	13534	1995	$28.00	Nostalgic Vinyl Series
Solo in the Spotlight replica (brunette)	13820	1995	$28.00	Nostalgic Vinyl Series
Something Extra	0863	1992	$30.00	Meijers
Sophisticated Lady	5313	1990	$220.00	Porcelain
Southern Beauty	3284	1991	$30.00	Winn Dixie
Southern Belle	1393	1988	$25.00	Sears
Southern Belle	2586	1991	$50.00	Sears
Southern Belle	11478	1994	$95.00	Great Eras Collection
Spanish	4031	1983	$140.00	Dolls of the World Series
Spanish	4963	1992	$75.00	Dolls of the World Series
Sparkle Eyes	2482	1992	$25.00	
Sparkle Eyes (black)	5940	1992	$15.00	
Sparkling Splendor	10994	1993	$45.00	Service Merchandise
Special Black Ponytail Club Outfit	N/A	1993	$500.00	You've Come A Long Way
Special Expressions	3197	1992	$25.00	Woolworth
Special Expressions	10048	1993	$25.00	Woolworth
Special Expressions (black)	3198	1992	$35.00	Woolworth
Special Expressions (black)	N/A	1993	$25.00	Woolworth
Special Expressions (Hispanic)	3200	1992	$20.00	Woolworth
Special Expressions (Hispanic)	10050	1993	$25.00	Woolworth
Special Expressions Mint Dress	2582	1991	$30.00	Woolworth
Special Expressions Mint Dress (black)	2583	1991	$30.00	Woolworth
Special Expressions Pink Dress	5504	1990	$30.00	Woolworth
Special Expressions Pink Dress (black)	5505	1990	$35.00	Woolworth
Special Expressions White Dress	4842	1989	$35.00	Woolworth
Special Expressions White Dress (black)	7326	1989	$35.00	Woolworth
Sport Star	1334	1979	$25.00	
Spots 'n Dots	10491	1993	$30.00	Toys 'R' Us
Spring Bouquet	3477	1992	$35.00	Supermarket
Spring Bouquet	12989	1995	$80.00	Enchanted Season
Spring Parade (black)	2257	1991	$45.00	Toys 'R' Us
Spring Parade Easter	7008	1991	$50.00	Toys 'R' Us

BARBIE® DOLLS

Listed Alphabetically

DOLL	NUMBER	YEAR	VALUE	STORE/COLLECTION
Standard	1190	1967	$318.00	
Standard	0850	1970	$250.00	
Standard (redhead)	1190	1967	$800.00	
Star Dream	4550	1987	$85.00	Sears
Starlight Splender	2703	1991	$750.00	Bob Mackie
Starlight Waltz	14070	1995	$90.00	
Sterling Wishes	3342	1991	$195.00	Spiegel
Straight Legs	1190	1967	N/A	
Strollin' Fun Barbie & Kelly	13742	1995	$20.00	
Strollin' Fun Barbie & Kelly (black)	13743	1995	$20.00	
Style Magic	1283	1989	$25.00	
Summit (Asian)	7029	1992	$30.00	
Summit (black)	7028	1992	$30.00	
Summit (blonde)	7027	1992	$30.00	
Summit (Hispanic)	7030	1990	$55.00	
Sun Gold (black)	7745	1985	$20.00	
Sun Gold Malibu	1067	1984	$20.00	
Sun Gold Malibu	1067	1986	$200.00	Barbie Doll Reunion
Sun Gold Malibu dressed as flower	1067	1988	$300.00	Barbie in Seattle
Sun Gold Malibu (Hispanic)	4970	1984	$15.00	
Sun Jewel	10953	1994	$10.00	
Sun Lovin' Malibu	1067	1979	$30.00	
Sun Sensation	1390	1992	$15.00	
Sun Set Malibu	1067	1971	N/A	
Sun Valley, The Sports Set (blonde)	7806	1973	$95.00	
Sunflower	13488	1995	$15.00	Toys 'R' Us
Sunsational Hispanic	4970	1984	$45.00	
Sunsational Malibu	1067	1982	$45.00	
Super Dance Barbie	5838	1982	$40.00	
Super Fashion Fireworks	N/A	1976	$75.00	
Super Fashion Fireworks #2	N/A	1976	$75.00	
Super Fashion Fireworks #3	N/A	1976	$75.00	
Super Hair (black)	3296	1987	$35.00	
Super Hair (blonde)	3101	1987	$35.00	
Super Size	9828	1977	$125.00	
Super Size Bridal	N/A	1978	$100.00	
Super Size with Super Hair	N/A	1979	$125.00	
Super Star	9720	1977	$75.00	
Super Star	2762	1987	N/A	Glamorous U.S. Barbie
Super Star	7965	1987	N/A	Glamorous U.S. Barbie

Barbie® Dolls

Listed Alphabetically

Doll	Number	Year	Value	Store/Collection
Super Star	9258	1987	N/A	Glamorous U.S. Barbie
Super Star	9259	1987	N/A	Glamorous U.S. Barbie
Super Star	9261	1987	N/A	Glamorous U.S. Barbie
Super Star	1604	1989	$50.00	
Super Star	10592	1993	$35.00	Wal-Mart
Super Star (1st issue with comb)	9720	1976	$125.00	
Super Star (2nd issue with necklace)	9720	1976	$100.00	
Super Star (black)	1605	1989	N/A	
Super Star (black)	10711	1993	$35.00	Wal-Mart
Super Star (Fashion Change-About)	N/A	1978	$55.00	
Super Star (In The Spotlight)	N/A	1978	$75.00	
Super Star (with Free Gift) #1	N/A	1977	$75.00	
Super Star (with Free Gift) #2	N/A	1977	$75.00	
Super Star (with Free Gift) #3	N/A	1977	$100.00	
Supertalk	N/A	1994	$40.00	
Supertalk (black)	N/A	1994	$40.00	
Swan Lake	1648	1991	$175.00	Ballet Series
Swedish	4032	1983	$95.00	Dolls of the World Series
Sweet 16 (blonde)	7796	1973	$75.00	
Sweet Dreams	13611	1995	Rtl	
Sweet Dreams (black)	13630	1995	Rtl	
Sweet Lavender	2522	1992	$20.00	Woolworth
Sweet Lavender (black)	3198	1992	$30.00	Woolworth
Sweet Lavender (Hispanic)	3200	1992	$30.00	Woolworth
Sweet Romance	2917	1991	$30.00	Toys 'R' Us
Sweet Roses	7635	1990	$40.00	Toys 'R' Us
Sweet Spring	3208	1991	$25.00	Supermarket
Swim 'n Dive	11505	1994	$20.00	
Swim 'n Dive (black)	11734	1994	$20.00	
Swirl Ponytail (ash blonde)	0850	1964	$550.00	
Swirl Ponytail (blonde)	0850	1964	$175.00	
Swirl Ponytail (brunette)	0850	1964	$550.00	
Swirl Ponytail (redhead)	0850	1964	$275.00	
Swiss	7541	1984	$85.00	Dolls of the World Series
Talking	1115	1968	$276.00	
Talking	1115	1969	$295.00	
Talking	1115	1971	$275.00	
Talking (auburn)	1115	1969	$295.00	
Talking (blonde)	1115	1969	$175.00	
Talking Busy (blonde)	1195	1971	$295.00	

BARBIE® DOLLS

Listed Alphabetically

DOLL	NUMBER	YEAR	VALUE	STORE/COLLECTION
Talking Busy (blonde)	3311	1972	$285.00	
Talking Busy "Holdin' Hands"	1195	1972	$295.00	
Talking Perfectly Plaid Set (auburn)	1193	1993	Rtl	Sears
Talking Ponytail (auburn)	1115	1967	$285.00	
Talking Ponytail (brunette)	1115	1967	$285.00	
Talking (Spanish)	8348	1968	$285.00	
Teacher	13194	1995	$25.00	
Teacher (black)	13195	1995	$25.00	
Teen Talk (ash blonde)	5745	1991	$80.00	
Teen Talk (black)	1612	1992	$50.00	
Teen Talk (blonde)	5745	1991	$80.00	
Teen Talk (brunette)	5745	1991	$80.00	
Teen Talk (redhead)	5745	1992	$35.00	
Teen Talk (strawberry blonde)	5745	1991	$80.00	
Ten Speeder	7777	1973	$13.00	
The Beach Party	1703	1981	$100.00	Department Store
The Beats Barbie	2751	1990	$25.00	
Theatre Elegance	12077	1994	$135.00	Spiegel
Toothfairy	11645	1994	$25.00	Wal-Mart
Totally Hair (black)	5948	1991	$30.00	
Totally Hair (blonde)	1112	1991	$20.00	
Totally Hair (brunette)	1117	1991	$30.00	
Trade In Barbie	1162	1967	$375.00	
Trail Blazin'	2783	1991	$25.00	Supermarket
Travel in Style Set (blonde)	1544	1967	$240.00	Sears
Treasures	N/A	1994	$65.00	Kraft
Troll	10257	1993	$15.00	
Tropical	1017	1986	$45.00	
Tropical (black)	1022	1986	$15.00	
Tropical (Hispanic)	1646	1986	$50.00	
Tropical Splash	12446	1995	$10.00	
Twinkle Lights (black)	N/A	1993	$30.00	
Twinkle Lights Pink	N/A	1993	$35.00	
Twirly Curls	5579	1983	$30.00	Department Store
Twirly Curls (black)	5723	1983	$30.00	
Twist 'n Turn #1 (Summer Sand)	1160	1967	$395.00	
Twist 'n Turn #2 (Chocolate Bon-Bon)	1160	1967	$395.00	
Twist 'n Turn #3 (Go-Go Co-Co)	1160	1967	$395.00	
Twist 'n Turn #4 (Sun Kissed)	1160	1967	$395.00	
Twist 'n Turn (auburn)	1160	1966	$450.00	

BARBIE® DOLLS

Listed Alphabetically

DOLL	NUMBER	YEAR	VALUE	STORE/COLLECTION
Twist 'n Turn (blonde)	1160	1966	$395.00	
Twist 'n Turn (brunette)	1160	1966	$395.00	
Twist 'n Turn (brunette)	1160	1969	$395.00	
Twist 'n Turn (brunette)	1160	1970	$395.00	
Twist 'n Turn (brunette)	1160	1971	$345.00	
Twist 'n Turn (redhead)	1160	1967	$600.00	
U. S. Olympic Wardrobe	9044	1975	95.00	Sears
Unicef	1920	1990	$35.00	
Unicef (Asian)	4774	1990	$30.00	
Unicef (black)	4770	1989	$35.00	
Unicef (Hispanic)	4782	1989	$25.00	
Uptown Chic	11623	1994	$75.00	Classique Collection
Vacation Sensation (blue)	1675	1986	$45.00	Toys 'R' Us
Vacation Sensation (pink)	1675	1988	$45.00	Toys 'R' Us
Valentine	12675	1994	$15.00	Special Edition
Very Violet	1859	1992	$95.00	Price Wholesale Club
Victorian Elegance	12579	1994	$110.00	Hallmark
Wacky Warehouse I	11763	1992	$65.00	Kool Aid
Wacky Warehouse II	1859	1994	$65.00	Kool Aid
Walk Lively (silver blonde)	1182	1972	$150.00	
Walking Miss America	3200	1972	N/A	
Wedding Day	2621	1989	$695.00	Porcelain
Wedding Day	9608	1991	$20.00	
Wedding Fantasy	2125	1990	$30.00	
Wedding Fantasy	2125	1991	$55.00	
Wedding Fantasy (black)	9638	1989	$43.00	
Wedding Fantasy (black)	7011	1990	$25.00	
Western	1757	1981	$30.00	
Western Fun	9932	1990	$25.00	
Western Fun (black)	2930	1990	$17.00	
Western Stampin'	10293	1993	$25.00	
Western Stampin' (black)	10539	1995	$20.00	
Wet 'n Wild	4103	1990	$25.00	
Wig Wardrobe	0871	1964	$295.00	
Wild Style	0411	1992	$30.00	Target
Winter Fantasy	5946	1990	$200.00	F.A.O. Schwarz
Winter Fun	5949	1990	$40.00	Toys 'R' Us
Winter Princess	10655	1993	$550.00	Princess Collection
Winter Royal	10658	1993	$95.00	Sam's Wholesale Club

BARBIE® Dolls

Listed by Stock Number

Number / Doll		Year	Value	Store/Collection
0411	Wild Style	1992	$30.00	Target
0850	Standard	1970	$250.00	
0850	Swirl Ponytail (ash blonde)	1964	$550.00	
0850	Swirl Ponytail (blonde)	1964	$175.00	
0850	Swirl Ponytail (brunette)	1964	$550.00	
0850	Swirl Ponytail (redhead)	1964	$275.00	
0863	Something Extra	1992	$30.00	
0871	Wig Wardrobe	1964	$295.00	
850	#1 Ponytail (blonde)	1959	$4200.00	
850	#1 Ponytail (brunette)	1959	$4600.00	
850	#2 Ponytail (blonde)	1959	$4000.00	
850	#2 Ponytail (brunette)	1959	$5100.00	
850	#3 Ponytail (blonde)	1960	$800.00	
850	#3 Ponytail (brunette)	1960	$798.00	
850	#4 Ponytail (blonde)	1960	$695.00	
850	#4 Ponytail (brunette)	1960	$250.00	
850	#5 Ponytail (brunette with arm tag)	1961	$412.00	
850	#5 Ponytail (lemon blonde with arm tag)	1961	$240.00	
850	#5 Ponytail (pale blonde with arm tag)	1961	$420.00	
850	#5 Ponytail (redhead with arm tag)	1961	$450.00	
850	#6 Bubble Cut (bright Titian)	1961	$850.00	
850	#6 Ponytail (ash blonde)	1962	$185.00	
850	#6 Ponytail (blonde)	1962	$245.00	
850	#6 Ponytail (brunette)	1962	$235.00	
850	#6 Ponytail (redhead)	1962	$195.00	
850	#6 Wheat Blonde	1962	$265.00	
850	#6 Yellow Blonde	1962	$195.00	
850	#7 Ponytail	1962	$150.00	
850	Bubble Cut (blonde)	1961	$225.00	
850	Bubble Cut (blonde)	1962	$200.00	
850	Bubble Cut (bright Titian)	1962	N/A	
850	Bubble Cut (brown)	1962	$200.00	
850	Bubble Cut (brownette)	1961	$750.00	
850	Bubble Cut (brunette)	1962	$200.00	
850	Bubble Cut (redhead)	1961	$225.00	
850	Bubble Cut (redhead)	1962	$200.00	
870	Fashion Queen (no wigs)	1963	$375.00	
870	Fashion Queen (with wigs)	1963	$550.00	
1017	Tropical	1986	$45.00	
1022	Tropical (black)	1986	$15.00	

Barbie® Dolls

Listed by Stock Number

Number / Doll		Year	Value	Store/Collection
1283	Style Magic	1989	$25.00	
1290	Beauty Secrets	1980	$300.00	Barbie Convention
1290	Beauty Secrets	1980	$45.00	
1292	Hispanic	1980	$95.00	
1293	Barbie Doll (black)	1980	$95.00	
1334	Sport Star	1979	$25.00	
1350	Animal Lovin'	1989	$35.00	
1364	Blue Rhapsody	1991	$275.00	Service Merchandise
1372	Fun To Dress (revised)	1989	$10.00	
1373	Fun To Dress (black, revised)	1989	$10.00	
1374	Frills & Fantasy	1988	$60.00	Wal-Mart
1390	Sun Sensation	1992	$15.00	
1393	Southern Belle	1988	$25.00	Sears
1429	Happy Holidays	1992	$120.00	Happy Holidays Collection
1434	Mermaid	1992	$15.00	
1490	Cool 'n Sassy	1992	$25.00	Toys 'R' Us
1511	Barbie Doll	1991	$300.00	McGlynns Bakery
1521	Benefit Ball	1992	$150.00	Classique Collection
1534	Barbie Doll (black)	1991	$250.00	McGlynns Bakery
1539	Madison Avenue	1991	$200.00	F.A.O. Schwarz
1544	Travel in Style Set (blonde)	1967	$240.00	Sears
1551	New Talking Dinner Dazzle Set (blonde)	1967	N/A	Sears
1585	Action Accents Set (auburn)	1969	$900.00	Sears
1585	Dramatic New Living Barbie	1971	$65.00	
1600	Parisian	1981	$150.00	Dolls of the World Series
1602	Italian	1981	$180.00	Dolls of the World Series
1604	Super Star	1989	$50.00	
1605	Super Star (black)	1989	N/A	
1612	Teen Talk (black)	1992	$50.00	
1623	Dream Bride Spec. Wedding Gown	1991	$30.00	Barbie Wedding Dreams
1646	Tropical (Hispanic)	1986	$50.00	
1647	Dream Glow (Hispanic)	1985	$70.00	
1648	Swan Lake	1991	$175.00	Ballet Series
1675	Vacation Sensation (blue)	1986	$45.00	Toys 'R' Us
1675	Vacation Sensation (pink)	1988	$45.00	Toys 'R' Us
1703	Happy Holidays	1988	$725.00	Happy Holidays Collection
1703	The Beach Party	1981	$100.00	Department Store
1708	Blue Rhapsody	1986	$900.00	Porcelain
1737	Jewel Secrets	1987	$35.00	
1738	Funtime & purple watch	1987	$30.00	

BARBIE® Dolls

Listed by Stock Number

NUMBER / DOLL		YEAR	VALUE	STORE/COLLECTION
1739	Funtime & black watch	1986	$30.00	
1753	Native American #1	1993	$45.00	Dolls of the World Series
1756	Jewel Secrets (black)	1987	$25.00	
1757	Horse Lovin'	1983	$45.00	
1757	Western	1981	$30.00	
1788	My First Ballerina	1987	$20.00	
1788	My First Barbie (bangs)	1985	$15.00	
1801	My First Ballerina (black)	1987	$25.00	
1801	My First Barbie (black)	1988	$16.00	
1858	Royal Romance	1992	$85.00	Sam's Wholesale Club
1859	Very Violet	1992	$95.00	Price Wholesale Club
1859	Wacky Warehouse II	1994	$65.00	Kool Aid
1861	Romantic Bride	1993	$30.00	
1865	Evening Flame	1991	$150.00	Home Shopping Club
1871	Happy Holidays	1991	$175.00	Happy Holidays Collection
1874	Golden Dreams (1st issue)	1981	$60.00	
1875	My First Barbie	1981	$20.00	
1875	My First Barbie	1984	$20.00	
1875	My First Barbie (2nd issue)	1983	$25.00	
1876	Party Perfect	1992	$45.00	Shopco/Venture
1879	Blue Elegance	1992	$30.00	Hill's
1880	Rollerskating	1981	$50.00	
1886	Satin Nights #1 (all white earrings)	1992	$95.00	Service Merchandise
1886	Satin Nights #2 (silver and white earrings)	1992	$95.00	Service Merchandise
1916	Russian	1989	$75.00	Dolls of the World Series
1917	Mexican	1989	$75.00	Dolls of the World Series
1920	Unicef	1990	$35.00	
1922	Gift Giving	1986	$20.00	
1922	Happy Birthday	1981	$75.00	
1922	Happy Birthday (2nd issue)	1983	$25.00	
1922	Happy Birthday (3rd issue)	1984	$20.00	
1953	Garden Party	1989	$20.00	
1981	Royal	1981	$180.00	Dolls of the World Series
2000	Case with Doll (Swirl Ponytail)	1966	$1000.00	
2001	Party Premiere	1992	$25.00	Supermarket
2017	Rockette	1992	$225.00	F.A.O. Schwarz
2066	Flight Time (Hispanic)	1990	$35.00	
2080	Friendship Barbie Berlin Wall II	1991	$70.00	
2125	Wedding Fantasy	1990	$30.00	
2125	Wedding Fantasy	1991	$55.00	

BARBIE® Dolls

Listed by Stock Number

NUMBER / DOLL		YEAR	VALUE	STORE/COLLECTION
2126	Magic Moves	1986	$15.00	
2127	Magic Moves (black)	1986	$35.00	
2210	Fashion Photo #1	1978	60.00	
2210	Fashion Photo #2	1978	$60.00	
2214	Rollerblade	1992	$16.00	
2242	Dream Glow (black)	1986	$40.00	
2248	Dream Glow	1986	$45.00	
2249	Home Pretty	1990	$25.00	
2256	Italian	1993	$35.00	Dolls of the World Series
2257	Spring Parade (black)	1991	$45.00	Toys 'R' Us
2282	Anniversary Star	1992	$40.00	Wal-Mart
2289	Hawaiian Superstar	1978	$400.00	
2308	Hollywood Hair	1993	$35.00	
2366	Jewel Jubilee	1991	$95.00	Sam's Wholesale Club
2374	Earring Magic (black)	1993	$20.00	
2396	Happy Holidays (black)	1992	$100.00	Happy Holidays Collection
2449	Astronaut	1986	$95.00	
2452	Denim 'n Lace	1992	$35.00	Ames
2482	Sparkle Eyes	1992	$25.00	
2516	My First Barbie	1993	$15.00	
2517	My Size	1992	$175.00	
2517	My Size	1993	$175.00	
2517	My Size	1994	$150.00	
2522	Sweet Lavender	1992	$20.00	Woolworth
2570	Fun To Dress (black)	1993	$10.00	
2582	Special Expressions Mint Dress	1991	$30.00	Woolworth
2583	Special Expressions Mint Dress (black)	1991	$30.00	Woolworth
2586	Southern Belle	1991	$50.00	Sears
2587	Golden Evening	1991	$40.00	Target
2597	Kissing (bangs style)	1980	$50.00	
2597	Kissing (extra dress)	1980	$45.00	Department Store
2597	Kissing (parted hair style)	1980	$45.00	
2598	Pretty Changes	1980	$35.00	
2621	Wedding Day	1989	$695.00	Porcelain
2696	Happy Holidays (black)	1991	$125.00	Happy Holidays Collection
2702	Enchanted Evening	1991	$45.00	J.C. Penney
2703	Starlight Splender	1991	$750.00	Bob Mackie
2704	Platinum	1991	$750.00	Bob Mackie
2713	Fashion Play (teal blue dress, eyes)	1991	$25.00	
2721	School Fun	1991	$20.00	Toys 'R' Us

BARBIE® Dolls

Listed by Stock Number

Number / Doll	Year	Value	Store/Collection
2730 Fashion Play	1992	N/A	
2751 Barbie and the Beats	1990	$25.00	
2751 The Beats Barbie	1990	$25.00	
2753 Malibu Fashion Combo	1978	$50.00	
2762 Super Star	1987	N/A	Glamorous U.S. Barbie
2763 Fun To Dress (Hispanic)	1993	$10.00	
2767 My First Barbie (black)	1993	$10.00	
2770 My First Barbie (Hispanic)	1993	$10.00	
2783 Trail Blazin'	1991	$25.00	Supermarket
2901 Pretty Hearts	1991	$30.00	Supermarket
2909 Party in Pink	1991	$35.00	Ames
2917 Sweet Romance	1991	$30.00	Toys 'R' Us
2921 Night Sensation	1991	$195.00	F.A.O. Schwarz
2930 Western Fun (black)	1990	$17.00	
2954 Cute 'n Cool	1991	$40.00	Target
2954 Dayton Hudson Cute 'n Cool	1991	$25.00	
2969 Royal Invitation	1993	$125.00	Spiegel
2995 Peruvian	1986	$75.00	Dolls of the World Series
2996 Deluxe Tropical	1985	$45.00	
2997 Greek	1986	$85.00	Dolls of the World Series
2998 Sears 100th Anniversary Celebration	1985	$75.00	Sears
3022 Cool Times	1989	$25.00	
3055 Rocker Dancin' Action	1987	$30.00	
3101 Super Hair (blonde)	1987	$35.00	
3117 Pretty in Purple	1992	$45.00	K-Mart
3121 Pretty in Purple (black)	1992	45.00	K-Mart
3137 American Beauty Queen	1991	$20.00	
3157 Caboodles	1993	$20.00	
3161 Red Romance	1992	$30.00	Supermarket
3188 German	1987	$110.00	Dolls of the World Series
3189 Icelandic	1987	$70.00	Dolls of the World Series
3192 Fantastica	1992	$55.00	Sam's Wholesale Club
3196 Fantastica	1992	$55.00	Pace Wholesale Club
3197 Special Expressions	1992	$25.00	Woolworth
3198 Special Expressions (black)	1992	$35.00	Woolworth
3198 Sweet Lavender (black)	1992	$30.00	Woolworth
3200 Special Expressions (Hispanic)	1992	$20.00	Woolworth
3200 Sweet Lavender (Hispanic)	1992	$30.00	Woolworth
3200 Walking Miss America	1972	N/A	
3208 Sweet Spring	1991	$25.00	Supermarket

Barbie® Dolls

Listed by Stock Number

Number / Doll		Year	Value	Store/Collection
3210	Montgomery Wards Anniversary Doll	1972	$425.00	Montgomery Wards
3237	Beach Blast	1989	$10.00	
3240	Fun To Dress	1993	$10.00	
3245	American Beauty Queen (black)	1991	$25.00	
3248	Rappin' Rockin'	1992	$30.00	
3262	Oriental	1981	$180.00	Dolls of the World Series
3263	Scottish	1981	$140.00	Dolls of the World Series
3269	Forget-Me-Nots	1972	N/A	Kellogg Company
3274	Evening Sparkle	1990	$45.00	Hill's
3284	Southern Beauty	1991	$30.00	Winn Dixie
3296	Super Hair (black)	1987	$35.00	
3303	Beautiful Blues Set (brunette)	1967	N/A	Sears
3311	Busy Barbie	1972	$150.00	
3311	Talking Busy (blonde)	1972	$285.00	
3342	Sterling Wishes	1991	$195.00	Spiegel
3360	Air Force	1991	$50.00	Stars N' Stripes
3388	Birthday Party	1993	$30.00	
3406	Holiday Doll	1991	$45.00	Applause
3412	Blossom Beauty	1991	$45.00	Shopco/Venture
3415	Enchanted Evening	1987	$475.00	Porcelain
3421	Feelin' Groovy	1986	$175.00	BillyBoy
3474	Fancy Frills Two Lovely Lingerie (pink)	1992	$40.00	
3477	Spring Bouquet	1992	$35.00	Supermarket
3509	Dance Club	1989	$30.00	
3523	Happy Holidays	1989	$275.00	Happy Holidays Collection
3533	Golden Dreams (2nd issue)	1981	$60.00	Department Store
3549	Moonlight Rose	1991	$40.00	Hill's
3550	Snap 'n Play	1992	$15.00	
3554	Pink & Pretty	1982	$40.00	
3556	Snap 'n Play (black)	1992	$15.00	
3596	Evening Enchantment	1989	$55.00	Sears
3602	Glitter Beach	1993	$25.00	
3677	Friendship Barbie Berlin Wall III	1992	$25.00	
3677	German Friendship	1991	$25.00	
3678	Ballroom Beauty	1991	$30.00	Wal-Mart
3679	Birthday Surprise	1992	$35.00	
3702	Gibson Girl	1993	$75.00	Great Eras Collection
3704	Miss Barbie with 3 wigs and swing	1964	N/A	Sears
3717	Funtime & blue watch	1987	$30.00	
3718	Funtime & pink watch	1987	$25.00	

Barbie® Dolls

Listed by Stock Number

Number / Doll		Year	Value	Store/Collection
3722	Barbie for President	1991	$50.00	Toys 'R' Us
3808	Picnic Pretty	1992	$30.00	Osco Drugs
3817	Blossom Beauty	1992	$280.00	Sears
3830	Bath Blast (black)	1993	$10.00	
3836	Secret Hearts (black)	1993	$25.00	
3839	My First Barbie	1992	$15.00	
3842	Fashion Play (black)	1992	N/A	
3850	Dr. Barbie	1988	$50.00	
3856	Magic Curl	1982	$30.00	
3860	Fashion Play (Hispanic)	1992	N/A	
3860	My First Barbie (Hispanic)	1992	$15.00	
3861	My First Barbie (black)	1992	$15.00	
3897	India	1983	$150.00	Dolls of the World Series
3898	Eskimo	1983	$120.00	Dolls of the World Series
3898	Eskimo Barbie in Indian costume	1982	$375.00	Michigan Entertains Barbie
3936	Army	1989	$35.00	American Beauty Collection
3939	25th Anniversary	1972	$600.00	Montgomery Wards
3940	Barbie For President (black)	1991	$50.00	Toys 'R' Us
3963	Lavender Looks	1989	$55.00	Wal-Mart
3966	Army (Dress Blues)	1990	$35.00	Stars 'n Stripes
3989	Magic Curl (black)	1982	$30.00	
4031	Spanish	1983	$140.00	Dolls of the World Series
4032	Swedish	1983	$95.00	Dolls of the World Series
4043	Hair Fair	1967	$90.00	
4044	Hair Fair (blonde)	1971	$175.00	
4051	Birthday Surprise (black)	1992	$20.00	
4061	Island Fun	1988	$25.00	
4063	Flapper	1993	$100.00	Great Eras Collection
4094	Hair Fair	1967	$90.00	
4098	Happy Holidays	1990	$150.00	Happy Holidays Collection
4103	Wet 'n Wild	1990	$25.00	
4110	Cool 'n Sassy (black)	1992	$25.00	Toys 'R' Us
4116	Regal Reflections	1992	$200.00	Spiegel
4159	Bath Blast	1993	$10.00	
4220	Quick Curl (blonde)	1972	$65.00	
4220	Quick Curl With extra outfit	1973	$65.00	Store Promotion
4247	Empress Bride	1992	$895.00	Bob Mackie
4248	Neptune Fantasy	1992	$950.00	Bob Mackie
4248	Neptune Fantasy face dressed magician	1994	$450.00	Magic of Barbie in Birmingham
4385	Disney Special (with mouse hat)	1991	$50.00	Children's Palace

Barbie® Dolls

Listed by Stock Number

Number / Doll		Year	Value	Store/Collection
7008	Spring Parade Easter	1991	$50.00	Toys 'R' Us
7009	Peach Blossom	1992	$45.00	Sam's Wholesale Club
7011	Wedding Fantasy (black)	1990	$25.00	
7014	Earring Magic (blonde)	1993	$20.00	
7025	Great Shapes	1984	$30.00	
7025	Great Shapes & Walkman®	1983	$30.00	
7027	Summit (blonde)	1992	$30.00	
7028	Summit (black)	1992	$30.00	
7029	Summit (Asian)	1992	$30.00	
7030	Summit (Hispanic)	1990	$55.00	
7057	Evening Elegance	1990	$85.00	J.C. Penney
7072	Loving You	1984	$25.00	
7072	Loving You in Red Silver Sensation	1984	$450.00	Barbie Loves New York
7080	Dance Magic (black)	1990	$20.00	
7123	Costume Ball	1991	$25.00	
7134	Costume Ball (black)	1991	$25.00	
7144	Fancy Frills Lingerie (European)	1989	$10.00	
7193	Fashion Play (pink & white jumpsuit)	1983	$25.00	
7233	Gold Medal Olympic Sports	1975	$75.00	
7233	Gold Medal U. S. Olympics	1976	$75.00	
7262	Gold Medal Skater	1975	$75.00	
7262	Gold Medal Skier	1976	$125.00	
7264	Gold Medal Skater	1976	$75.00	
7264	Gold Medal Skier	1975	$75.00	
7270	Free Movin' (blonde)	1974	$65.00	
7270	Free Moving	1976	$75.00	
7272	Barbie & Snowball Her Pet Dog	1990	$18.00	
7326	Special Expressions White Dress (black)	1989	$35.00	Woolworth
7329	Malaysian	1991	$35.00	Dolls of the World Series
7330	Czechoslovakian	1991	$110.00	Dolls of the World Series
7335	Dream Fantasy	1990	$50.00	Wal-Mart
7344	Australian	1993	$22.00	Dolls of the World Series
7365	Ice Capades	1990	$45.00	
7348	Ice Capades (black)	1990	$35.00	
7373	Fun To Dress (Hispanic)	1993	$10.00	
7376	Nigerian	1990	$55.00	Dolls of the World Series
7470	Hawaiian	1975	$50.00	Department Store
7470	Hawaiian #1 (one-piece swimsuit)	1981	$40.00	Department Store
7470	Hawaiian #2 (two-piece swimsuit)	1983	$40.00	Department Store
7476	Gold and Lace	1989	$45.00	Target

BARBIE® Dolls

Listed by Stock Number

NUMBER / DOLL		YEAR	VALUE	STORE/COLLECTION
7511	Ski Fun	1991	$30.00	
7517	Irish	1984	$135.00	Dolls of the World Series
7526	Plantation Belle	1992	$250.00	Porcelain
7541	Swiss	1984	$85.00	Dolls of the World Series
7549	Marine	1992	$25.00	Stars 'n Stripes
7594	Marine (black)	1992	$25.00	Stars 'n Stripes
7613	Solo in the Spotlight	1990	$295.00	Porcelain
7635	Sweet Roses	1990	$40.00	Toys 'R' Us
7637	Party Pink	1989	$15.00	Winn Dixie
7668	Fun To Dress (black)	1988	$10.00	
7669	Lilac and Lovely	1987	$55.00	Sears
7734	Golden Greetings	1989	$225.00	F.A.O. Schwarz
7745	Sun Gold (black)	1985	$20.00	
7777	Ten Speeder	1973	$13.00	
7796	Sweet 16 (blonde)	1973	$75.00	
7806	Sun Valley, The Sports Set (blonde)	1973	$95.00	
7807	Newport #1	1974	$200.00	
7807	Newport #2	1974	$200.00	
7807	Newport, The Sports Set (blonde)	1973	$175.00	
7834	Great Shapes (black)	1984	$25.00	
7882	Fashion Bright	1992	$25.00	Toys 'R' Us
7902	Secret Hearts	1993	$20.00	
7913	Happy Birthday	1991	$40.00	
7926	Peaches 'n Cream	1985	$25.00	
7929	Day-To-Night	1985	$35.00	
7944	Day-To-Night (Hispanic)	1985	$30.00	
7945	Day-To-Night (black)	1985	$25.00	
7948	Birthday Party (black)	1993	30.00	
7951	Bath Magic (black)	1992	$12.00	
7965	Super Star	1987	N/A	Glamorous U.S. Barbie
8348	Talking (Spanish)	1968	$285.00	
8414	Posable	1965	N/A	Montgomery Wards
9025	Party Sensation	1990	$35.00	Sam's Wholesale Club
9042	Gold Medal Winter Sports	1975	$50.00	
9044	U. S. Olympic Wardrobe	1975	95.00	Sears
9049	Lavender Surprise	1989	$45.00	Sears
9093	Ballerina	1979	$50.00	
9093	Ballerina	1980	$50.00	Mervyn's
9093	Ballerina (1st issue)	1976	$25.00	
9093	Ballerina (2nd issue)	1976	$25.00	

NUMBER / DOLL	
9858	My First
9907	Beautiful
9916	Flight Ti
9932	Western
9942	My First
9943	My First
9943	My First
9943	My First
9943	My First
9944	My First
9973	Gay Pari
9973	Gay Pari
9973	Gay Pari
9973	Gay Pari
9988	Music Lo
10039	Paint &
10048	Special
10050	Special
10051	Shoppin
10057	Paint &
10058	Paint &
10059	Paint &
10123	Little D
10149	City Styl
10201	Crystal
10202	Golf Da
10246	Gold Se
10247	Disney
10255	Earring
10257	Troll
10280	Holiday
10292	Enchan
10293	Western
10339	Festiva
10412	Live Ac
10491	Spots '
10507	Love to
10522	Founta
10539	Wester
10592	Super S

BARBIE® Dolls

Listed by Stock Number

NUMBER	
9093	B
9093	B
9094	B
9099	B
9102	B
9180	D
9217	D
9258	S
9259	S
9261	S
9404	B
9423	A
9481	J
9481	J
9516	P
9561	H
9584	F
9588	L
9599	B
9599	B
9601	B
9603	B
9608	B
9608	V
9629	F
9638	V
9693	N
9694	N
9720	S
9720	S
9720	S
9725	L
9823	P
9828	S
9835	I
9843	F
9844	F
9845	S
9847	I
9858	N

NUMBER / DOLL		YEAR	VALUE	STORE/COLLECTION
10610	Angel Lights	1993	$125.00	
10655	Winter Princess	1993	$550.00	Christmas
10658	Winter Royal	1993	$95.00	Princess Collection
10684	Golden Winter	1993	$95.00	Sam's Wholesale Club
10688	Police Officer	1993	$31.00	J.C. Penney
10711	Super Star (black)	1993	$35.00	Toys 'R' Us
10713	Dream Wedding (black)	1993	$45.00	Wal-Mart
10776	Dress 'n Fun	1994	$6.00	
10803	Masquerade Ball	1993	$350.00	
10824	Happy Holidays	1993	$135.00	Bob Mackie
10911	Happy Holidays (black)	1993	$120.00	Happy Holidays Collection
10950	Royal Splendor	1993	$375.00	Happy Holidays Collection
10953	Sun Jewel	1994	$10.00	Porcelain
10963	Locket Surprise	1994	$14.00	
10965	Glitter Hair (blonde)	1994	$12.00	
10966	Glitter Hair (burnette)	1994	$12.00	
10968	Glitter Hair (redhead)	1994	$12.00	
10994	Sparkling Splendor	1993	$45.00	Service Merchandise
11074	Camp	1994	$12.00	
11079	Bedtime	1994	$15.00	
11099	Silken Flame (blonde)	1993	$750.00	Disney
11102	Dress 'n Fun (Hispanic)	1994	$6.00	
11104	Dutch	1994	$24.00	Dolls of the World Series
11160	Dr. Barbie (brunette)	1994	$250.00	Mattel Festival Doll
11160	Dr. Barbie (white with black baby)	1994	$50.00	Toys 'R' Us
11180	Chinese	1993	$24.00	Dolls of the World Series
11181	Kenyan	1994	$25.00	Dolls of the World Series
11184	Bedtime (black)	1994	$15.00	
11224	Locket Surprise (black)	1994	$14.00	
11276	Easter Fun	1993	$45.00	Supermarket
11294	My First Barbie	1994	$10.00	
11305	Silver Starlight	1992	$450.00	Porcelain
11332	Glitter Hair (black)	1994	$12.00	
11333	Birthday	1994	$25.00	
11334	Birthday (black)	1994	$25.00	
11340	My First Barbie (black)	1994	$10.00	
11341	My First Barbie (Hispanic)	1994	$10.00	
11342	My First Barbie (Asian)	1994	$10.00	
11397	Egyptian Queen	1994	$100.00	Great Eras Collection
11478	Southern Belle	1994	$95.00	Great Eras Collection

BARBIE® Dolls

Listed by Stock Number

Number / Doll		Year	Value	Store/Collection
11505	Swim 'n Dive	1994	$20.00	
11552	Air Force (Thunderbirds)	1994	$75.00	
11581	Barbie & Ken Thunderbirds (Air Force)	1993	$40.00	Stars 'n Stripes
11589	35th Anniversary Nostalgic (blonde)	1994	$25.00	
11609	Native American #2	1994	$24.00	Dolls of the World Series
11622	Evening Extravaganza (pink)	1994	$95.00	Classique Collection
11623	Uptown Chic	1994	$75.00	Classique Collection
11637	Evening Extravaganza (yellow)	1994	$95.00	Classique Collection
11645	Toothfairy	1994	$25.00	Wal-Mart
11652	Silver Screen	1993	$150.00	F.A.O. Schwarz
11689	Bicyclin'	1994	$30.00	
11734	Swim 'n Dive (black)	1994	$20.00	
11763	Wacky Warehouse I	1992	$65.00	Kool Aid
11782	35th Anniversary Nostalgic (brunette)	1994	$45.00	
11814	Dr. Barbie (black with white baby)	1994	$50.00	Toys 'R' Us
11817	Bicyclin' (black)	1994	$25.00	
11875	Snow Princess	1994	$135.00	Enchanted Season
11902	Dance 'n Twirl	1994	$55.00	
11902	Dream Dancing	1994	Rtl	
11921	Gymnast (brunette)	1994	$250.00	Mattel Festival Doll
12005	City Sophisticate	1994	$95.00	Service Merchandise
12009	Gold Jubilee	1994	$1400.00	Jubilee Series
12045	Scarlett Green Velvet (1st in series)	1994	$95.00	Hollywood Legends
12046	Queen of Hearts	1994	$230.00	Bob Mackie
12052	My Size Bride	1994	$175.00	
12053	My Size Bride (black)	1994	$150.00	
12077	Theatre Elegance	1994	$135.00	Spiegel
12097	Country & Western Star	1994	$30.00	Wal-Mart
12123	Evergreen Princess	1994	$135.00	Princess Collection
12127	Gymnast	1994	$14.00	
12143	Dance 'n Twirl (black)	1994	$50.00	
12143	Dream Dancing (black)	1994	Rtl	
12143	Dress 'n Fun (black)	1994	$6.00	
12149	Astronaut	1994	$35.00	Toys 'R'Us
12150	Astronaut (black)	1994	$45.00	Toys'R' Us
12152	Savy Shopper	1994	$175.00	Bloomingdale's
12153	Gymnast (black)	1994	$14.00	
12155	Happy Holidays	1994	$175.00	Happy Holidays Collection
12155	Happy Holidays	1994	$650.00	Mattel Festival Doll
12191	Night Dazzle	1994	$65.00	J.C. Penney

BARBIE® Dolls

Listed by Stock Number

NUMBER / DOLL		YEAR	VALUE	STORE/COLLECTION
12191	Night Dazzle	1994	$650.00	Mattel Festival Doll
12192	Holiday Dreams	1994	$35.00	Supermarket
12196	Happy Holidays (black)	1994	$125.00	Happy Holidays Collection
12243	Party Time	1994	$23.00	Toys 'R' Us
12322	Emerald Elegance	1994	$40.00	Toys 'R' Us
12323	Emerald Elegance (black)	1994	$30.00	Toys 'R' Us
12384	Season's Greetings	1994	$125.00	Sam's Wholesale Club
12410	Silver Sweetheart	1994	$55.00	Sears
12412	Polly Pockets	1994	$40.00	Hill's
12433	Ruffle Fun	1994	$12.00	
12434	Ruffle Fun (black)	1994	$12.00	
12435	Ruffle Fun (Hispanic)	1994	$12.00	
12443	Bubble Angel	1995	$12.00	
12444	Bubble Angel (black)	1995	$12.00	
12446	Tropical Splash	1995	$10.00	
12577	Pilgrim	1995	$23.00	American Stories Series
12578	Colonial	1995	$25.00	American Stories Series
12579	Victorian Elegance	1994	$110.00	Hallmark
12639	Cut 'n Style #1 (blonde)	1994	$12.00	
12642	Cut 'n Style #2 (black)	1994	$12.00	
12643	Cut 'n Style (brunette)	1994	$12.00	
12644	Cut 'n Style (redhead)	1994	$12.00	
12675	Valentine	1994	$15.00	Special Edition
12680	Pioneer	1995	$23.00	American Stories Series
12696	Slumber Party	1994	$14.00	
12697	Slumber Party (black)	1994	$14.00	
12698	German	1995	$24.00	Dolls of the World Series
12699	Native American #3	1995	$24.00	Dolls of the World Series
12700	Polynesian	1995	$24.00	Dolls of the World Series
12701	Dorothy (Wizard of Oz)	1995	$50.00	Hollywood Legends
12749	Shopping Spree	1994	$25.00	F.A.O. Schwarz
12791	Medieval Lady	1995	$50.00	Great Eras Collection
12792	Elizabethan Queen	1995	$50.00	Great Eras Collection
12815	Scarlett in Red Dress	1995	$85.00	Hollywood Legends
12905	Snow Princess (brunette)	1994	$1800.00	Mattel Festival Doll
12954	Birthday	1995	$20.00	
12955	Birthday (black)	1995	$25.00	
12989	Spring Bouquet	1995	$80.00	Enchanted Season
12997	Scarlett in BBQ Dress	1995	$85.00	Hollywood Legends
12998	Irish	1995	$24.00	Dolls of the World Series

Barbie® Dolls

Listed by Stock Number

Number / Doll		Year	Value	Store/Collection
12999	Midnight Gala	1995	$60.00	Classique Collection
13016	Rapunzel	1995	$40.00	Children's Collector Series
13051	Butterfly Princess	1995	$22.00	
13052	Butterfly Princess (black)	1995	$22.00	
13064	My First Princess	1995	$10.00	
13065	My First Princess (black)	1995	$10.00	
13066	My First Princess (Hispanic)	1995	$10.00	
13067	My First Princess (Asian)	1995	$10.00	
13083	Dance Moves	1995	$15.00	
13086	Dance Moves (black)	1995	$15.00	
13168	Christian Dior No. 1	1995	$175.00	Designer Collection
13173	Evergreen Princess (redhead)	1994	$650.00	Walt Disney Convention
13194	Teacher	1995	$25.00	
13195	Teacher (black)	1995	$25.00	
13199	Baywatch	1995	$20.00	
13238	Butterfly Princess (Hispanic)	1995	$22.00	
13239	Pog Barbie	1994	$15.00	Toys 'R' Us
13253	Birthday (Hispanic)	1995	$25.00	
13254	Scarlett in Black & White (New Orleans)	1995	$85.00	Hollywood Legends
13255	Sapphire Dreams	1995	$60.00	Toys 'R' Us
13257	Circus Star	1995	$90.00	F.A.O. Schwarz
13258	Baywatch (black)	1995	$20.00	
13472	Fire Fighter (black)	1995	$30.00	Toys 'R' Us
13488	Sunflower	1995	$15.00	Toys 'R' Us
13511	Hot Skatin'	1995	$12.00	
13512	Hot Skatin' (black)	1995	Rtl	
13534	Solo in the Spotlight replica (blonde)	1995	$28.00	Nostalgic Vinyl Series
13553	Fire Fighter	1995	$30.00	Toys 'R' Us
13554	Purple Passion (black)	1995	$30.00	Toys 'R' Us
13555	Purple Passion	1995	$30.00	Toys 'R' Us
13598	Peppermint Princess	1995	$60.00	Princess Collection
13611	Pretty Dreams	1995	$20.00	
13611	Sweet Dreams	1995	Rtl	
13614	Country Bride	1995	$12.00	Wal-Mart
13630	Sweet Dreams (black)	1995	Rtl	
13630	Pretty Dreams (black)	1995	$20.00	
13676	Maria (Sound of Music)	1995	$50.00	Hollywood Legends
13741	Schooltime Fun	1995	$20.00	Supermarket
13742	Strollin' Fun Barbie & Kelly	1995	$20.00	
13743	Strollin' Fun Barbie & Kelly (black)	1995	$20.00	

Barbie® Dolls

Listed by Stock Number

Number / Doll		Year	Value	Store/Collection
13767	My Size Princess Ballerina	1995	$175.00	
13768	My Size Princess Ballerina (black)	1995	$175.00	
13820	Solo in the Spotlight replica (brunette)	1995	$28.00	Nostalgic Vinyl Series
13938	Sing & Dance (black)	1995	Rtl	
13939	Dolls of the World Set	1995	$75.00	Dolls of the World Series
13940	Sea Pearl Mermaid	1995	$25.00	Hill's
14009	Shopping Chic	1995	$65.00	Spiegel
14030	Flying Hero	1995	$15.00	
14056	Goddess of the Sun	1995	$225.00	Bob Mackie
14061	Jeweled Splendor	1995	$400.00	F.A.O. Schwarz
14070	Starlight Waltz	1995	$90.00	
14106	Holiday Memories	1995	$50.00	Hallmark
14123	Happy Holidays	1995	$29.00	Happy Holidays Collection
14124	Happy Holidays (black)	1995	$29.00	Happy Holidays Collection
14309	Dr. Barbie (with 3 babies)	1995	$20.00	
14311	Holiday Jewel	1995	$190.00	Holiday Porcelain Series
14452	Bloomingdale's Donna Karan New York (brunette)	1995	$110.00	Bloomingdale's
14473	Pretty Hearts	1995	$5.00	
14479	Mattel 50th Anniversary Porcelain	1995	$700.00	Mattel Anniversary Doll
14545	Bloomingdale's Donna Karan New York (blonde)	1995	$95.00	Bloomingdale's
37028	Enchanted Evening	1987	$550.00	

BARBIE® DOLLS

Listed by Year

YEAR / DOLL	NUMBER	VALUE	STORE/COLLECTION
1959 #1 Ponytail (blonde)	850	$4200.00	
1959 #1 Ponytail (brunette)	850	$4600.00	
1959 #2 Ponytail (blonde)	850	$4000.00	
1959 #2 Ponytail (brunette)	850	$5100.00	
1960 #3 Ponytail (blonde)	850	$800.00	
1960 #3 Ponytail (brunette)	850	$798.00	
1960 #4 Ponytail (blonde)	850	$695.00	
1960 #4 Ponytail (brunette)	850	$250.00	
1961 #5 Ponytail (brunette with arm tag)	850	$412.00	
1961 #5 Ponytail (lemon blonde with arm tag)	850	$240.00	
1961 #5 Ponytail (pale blonde with arm tag)	850	$420.00	
1961 #5 Ponytail (redhead with arm tag)	850	$450.00	
1961 #6 Bubble Cut (bright Titian)	850	$850.00	
1961 Bubble Cut (blonde)	850	$225.00	
1961 Bubble Cut (brownette)	850	$750.00	
1961 Bubble Cut (redhead)	850	$225.00	
1962 #6 Ponytail (ash blonde)	850	$185.00	
1962 #6 Ponytail (blonde)	850	$245.00	
1962 #6 Ponytail (brunette)	850	$235.00	
1962 #6 Ponytail (redhead)	850	$195.00	
1962 #6 Wheat Blonde	850	$265.00	
1962 #6 Yellow Blonde	850	$195.00	
1962 #7 Ponytail	850	$150.00	
1962 Bubble Cut (blonde)	850	$200.00	
1962 Bubble Cut (bright Titian)	850	N/A	
1962 Bubble Cut (brown)	850	$200.00	
1962 Bubble Cut (brunette)	850	$200.00	
1962 Bubble Cut (redhead)	850	$200.00	
1963 Fashion Queen (no wigs)	870	$375.00	
1963 Fashion Queen (with wigs)	870	$550.00	
1964 Miss Barbie (Sleep Eye)	1060	$1500.00	
1964 Miss Barbie with 3 wigs and swing	3704	N/A	Sears
1964 Miss Barbie (Bendable Leg)	1060	N/A	
1964 Swirl Ponytail (ash blonde)	0850	$550.00	
1964 Swirl Ponytail (blonde)	0850	$175.00	
1964 Swirl Ponytail (brunette)	0850	$550.00	
1964 Swirl Ponytail (redhead)	0850	$275.00	
1964 Wig Wardrobe	0871	$295.00	
1965 American Girl (Bendable Leg)	1070	$80.00	
1965 American Girl (Bendable Leg, Side Part)	1070	$3300.00	

BARBIE® DOLLS

Listed by Year

YEAR / DOLL	NUMBER	VALUE	STORE/COLLECTION
1965 American Girl (blonde)	1070	$1650.00	
1965 American Girl (brown)	1070	$295.00	
1965 American Girl (brunette)	1070	$1195.00	
1965 American Girl (pale blonde)	1070	$750.00	
1965 American Girl (redhead)	1070	$325.00	
1965 Barbie Doll (Side Part)	N/A	N/A	
1965 Bendable Leg (American Girl style)	1070	$500.00	
1965 Bendable Leg (Bubble Cut)	1070	$1300.00	
1965 Bendable Leg (Side Part Flip)	1070	$2995.00	
1965 Color Magic (black turns red)	1150	$1850.00	
1965 Posable	8414	N/A	Montgomery Wards
1966 American Girl (Bend. Leg, Color Magic Face)	1070	$1350.00	
1966 American Girl (Bendable Leg)	1070	$1125.00	
1966 Barbie Doll (auburn)	N/A	N/A	
1966 Barbie Doll (Blonde)	N/A	N/A	
1966 Barbie Doll (brunette)	N/A	N/A	
1966 Case with Doll (Swirl Ponytail)	2000	$1000.00	
1966 Color Magic (cardboard box, blonde)	1150	$1400.00	
1966 Color Magic (cardboard box, midnight black)	1150	$1100.00	
1966 Color Magic (plastic box, blonde)	1150	$1100.00	
1966 Color Magic (plastic box, midnight black)	1150	$1500.00	
1966 Twist 'n Turn (auburn)	1160	$450.00	
1966 Twist 'n Turn (blonde)	1160	$395.00	
1966 Twist 'n Turn (brunette)	1160	$395.00	
1967 Barbie Doll	1070	N/A	
1967 Barbie Doll (standard)	1190	$350.00	
1967 Beautiful Blues Set (brunette)	3303	N/A	Sears
1967 Hair Fair	4043	$90.00	
1967 Hair Fair	4094	$90.00	
1967 New Talking Dinner Dazzle Set (blonde)	1551	N/A	Sears
1967 Standard	1190	$318.00	
1967 Standard (redhead)	1190	$800.00	
1967 Straight Legs	1190	N/A	
1967 Talking Ponytail (auburn)	1115	$285.00	
1967 Talking Ponytail (brunette)	1115	$285.00	
1967 Trade In Barbie	1162	$375.00	
1967 Travel in Style Set (blonde)	1544	$240.00	Sears
1967 Twist 'n Turn #1 (Summer Sand)	1160	$395.00	
1967 Twist 'n Turn #2 (Chocolate Bon-Bon)	1160	$395.00	
1967 Twist 'n Turn #3 (Go-Go Co-Co)	1160	$395.00	

BARBIE® DOLLS

Listed by Year

YEAR / DOLL	NUMBER	VALUE	STORE/COLLECTION
1967 Twist 'n Turn #4 (Sun Kissed)	1160	$395.00	
1967 Twist 'n Turn (redhead)	1160	$600.00	
1968 Talking	1115	$276.00	
1968 Talking (Spanish)	8348	$285.00	
1969 Action Accents Set (auburn)	1585	$900.00	Sears
1969 Barbie Doll (brunette)	1190	N/A	
1969 Talking	1115	$295.00	
1969 Talking (auburn)	115	$295.00	
1969 Talking (blonde)	1115	$175.00	
1969 Twist 'n Turn (brunette)	1160	$395.00	
1970 Barbie Doll (new swimsuit)	1190	$365.00	
1970 Living	1116	$175.00	
1970 New Living (auburn)	1116	$225.00	
1970 New Living (blonde)	1116	$225.00	
1970 Standard	0850	$250.00	
1970 Twist 'n Turn (brunette)	1160	$395.00	
1971 Dramatic New Living Barbie	1585	$65.00	
1971 Growin' Pretty Hair	1144	$233.00	
1971 Hair Fair (blonde)	4044	$175.00	
1971 Hair's Happening (auburn)	1174	$895.00	
1971 Live Action On Stage	1152	$233.00	
1971 Live Action (ranch)	10412	$150.00	Montgomery Wards
1971 Live Action (silver blonde)	1155	$115.00	
1971 Sun Set Malibu	1067	N/A	
1971 Talking	1115	$275.00	
1971 Talking Busy (blonde)	1195	$295.00	
1971 Twist 'n Turn (brunette)	1160	$345.00	
1972 25th Anniversary	3939	$600.00	Montgomery Wards
1972 Busy Barbie	3311	$150.00	
1972 Forget-Me-Nots	3269	N/A	Kellogg Company
1972 Growin' Pretty Hair	1144	$235.00	Sears
1972 Montgomery Wards Anniversary Doll	3210	$425.00	Montgomery Wards
1972 Quick Curl (blonde)	4220	$65.00	
1972 Talking Busy (blonde)	3311	$285.00	
1972 Talking Busy "Holdin' Hands"	1195	$295.00	
1972 Walk Lively (silver blonde)	1182	$150.00	
1972 Walking Miss America	3200	N/A	
1973 Live Action (plastic bag)	1155	$165.00	
1973 Newport, The Sports Set (blonde)	7807	$175.00	
1973 Quick Curl With extra outfit	4220	$65.00	Store Promotion

Barbie® Dolls

Listed by Year

Year / Doll		Number	Value	Store/Collection
1973	Sun Valley, The Sports Set (blonde)	7806	$95.00	
1973	Sweet 16 (blonde)	7796	$75.00	
1973	Ten Speeder	7777	$13.00	
1974	Free Movin' (blonde)	7270	$65.00	
1974	Newport #1	7807	$200.00	
1974	Newport #2	7807	$200.00	
1975	Gold Medal Olympic Sports	7233	$75.00	
1975	Gold Medal Skater	7262	$75.00	
1975	Gold Medal Skier	7264	$75.00	
1975	Gold Medal Winter Sports	9042	$50.00	
1975	Hawaiian	7470	$50.00	Department Store
1975	Malibu Barbie	1067	$45.00	
1975	U. S. Olympic Wardrobe	9044	95.00	Sears
1976	Ballerina (1st issue)	9093	$25.00	
1976	Ballerina (2nd issue)	9093	$25.00	
1976	Ballerina on Tour	9093	$175.00	Department Store
1976	Beautiful Bride	9599	$300.00	Department Store
1976	Beautiful Bride	9599	$75.00	
1976	Deluxe Quick Curl (Jergens)	9217	$60.00	
1976	Free Moving	7270	$75.00	
1976	Gold Medal Skater	7264	$75.00	
1976	Gold Medal Skier	7262	$125.00	
1976	Gold Medal U. S. Olympics	7233	$75.00	
1976	Malibu (Baggie)	N/A	$20.00	
1976	Plus 3	N/A	$75.00	Ben Franklin
1976	Super Fashion Fireworks	N/A	$75.00	
1976	Super Fashion Fireworks #2	N/A	$75.00	
1976	Super Fashion Fireworks #3	N/A	$75.00	
1976	Super Star (1st issue with comb)	9720	$125.00	
1976	Super Star (2nd issue with necklace)	9720	$100.00	
1977	Super Size	9828	$125.00	
1977	Super Star	9720	$75.00	
1977	Super Star (with Free Gift) #1	N/A	$75.00	
1977	Super Star (with Free Gift) #2	N/A	$75.00	
1977	Super Star (with Free Gift) #3	N/A	$100.00	
1978	Ballerina on Tour (reissue)	9093	$60.00	
1978	Beautiful Bride	9907	$200.00	
1978	Fashion Photo #1	2210	60.00	
1978	Fashion Photo #2	2210	$60.00	
1978	Hawaiian Superstar	2289	$400.00	

BARBIE® DOLLS

Listed by Year

YEAR / DOLL	NUMBER	VALUE	STORE/COLLECTION
1978 Malibu Fashion Combo	2753	$50.00	
1978 Super Size Bridal	N/A	$100.00	
1978 Super Star (Fashion Change-About)	N/A	$55.00	
1978 Super Star (In The Spotlight)	N/A	$75.00	
1979 Ballerina	9093	$50.00	
1979 Sport Star	1334	$25.00	
1979 Sun Lovin' Malibu	1067	$30.00	
1979 Super Size with Super Hair	N/A	$125.00	
1980 Ballerina	9093	$50.00	Mervyn's
1980 Barbie Doll (black)	1293	$95.00	
1980 Beauty Secrets	1290	$300.00	Barbie Convention
1980 Beauty Secrets	1290	$45.00	
1980 Hispanic	1292	$95.00	
1980 Kissing (bangs style)	2597	$50.00	
1980 Kissing (extra dress)	2597	$45.00	Department Store
1980 Kissing (parted hair style)	2597	$45.00	
1980 Pretty Changes	2598	$35.00	
1981 Golden Dreams (1st issue)	1874	$60.00	
1981 Golden Dreams (2nd issue)	3533	$60.00	Department Store
1981 Happy Birthday	1922	$75.00	
1981 Hawaiian #1 (one-piece swimsuit)	7470	$40.00	Department Store
1981 Italian	1602	$180.00	Dolls of the World Series
1981 My First Barbie	1875	$20.00	
1981 Oriental	3262	$180.00	Dolls of the World Series
1981 Parisian	1600	$150.00	Dolls of the World Series
1981 Rollerskating	1880	$50.00	
1981 Royal	1981	$180.00	Dolls of the World Series
1981 Scottish	3263	$140.00	Dolls of the World Series
1981 The Beach Party	1703	$100.00	Department Store
1981 Western	1757	$30.00	
1982 Eskimo Barbie in Indian costume	3898	$375.00	Michigan Entertains Barbie
1982 Fashion Jeans	5315	$45.00	
1982 Magic Curl	3856	$30.00	
1982 Magic Curl (black)	3989	$30.00	
1982 Pink & Pretty	3554	$40.00	
1982 Pink & Pretty Modeling Set	5239	$88.00	
1982 Sunsational Malibu	1067	$45.00	
1982 Super Dance Barbie	5838	$40.00	
1983 Angel Face	5640	$50.00	
1983 Ballerina	4983	$75.00	

BARBIE® DOLLS

Listed by Year

YEAR / DOLL		NUMBER	VALUE	STORE/COLLECTION
1993	Earring Magic (blonde)	7014	$20.00	
1993	Earring Magic (brunette)	10255	$20.00	
1993	Easter Fun	11276	$45.00	Supermarket
1993	Enchanted Princess	10292	$80.00	Sears
1993	Festiva	10339	$45.00	Sam's Wholesale Club
1993	Flapper	4063	$100.00	Great Eras Collection
1993	Fountain Mermaid (black)	10522	$15.00	
1993	Fun To Dress	3240	$10.00	
1993	Fun To Dress (black)	2570	$10.00	
1993	Fun To Dress (Hispanic)	2763	$10.00	
1993	Fun To Dress (Hispanic)	7373	$10.00	
1993	Gibson Girl	3702	$75.00	Great Eras Collection
1993	Glitter Beach	3602	$25.00	
1993	Gold Sensation	10246	$450.00	Porcelain
1993	Golden Winter	10684	$95.00	J.C. Penney
1993	Golf Date	10202	$25.00	Target
1993	Happy Holidays	10824	$135.00	Happy Holidays Collection
1993	Happy Holidays (black)	10911	$120.00	Happy Holidays Collection
1993	Hollywood Hair	2308	$35.00	
1993	Italian	2256	$35.00	Dolls of the World Series
1993	Love to Read	10507	$30.00	Toys 'R' Us
1993	Malt Shop	4581	$25.00	Toys 'R' Us
1993	Masquerade Ball	10803	$350.00	Bob Mackie
1993	Moonlight Magic (ethnic)	N/A	$50.00	Toys 'R' Us
1993	My First Barbie	2516	$15.00	
1993	My First Barbie (black)	2767	$10.00	
1993	My First Barbie (Hispanic)	2770	$10.00	
1993	My Size	2517	$175.00	
1993	Native American #1	1753	$45.00	Dolls of the World Series
1993	Opening Night	N/A	$95.00	Classique Collection
1993	Paint & Dazzle (black)	10058	$20.00	
1993	Paint & Dazzle (blonde)	10039	$20.00	
1993	Paint & Dazzle (brunette)	10059	$20.00	
1993	Paint & Dazzle (redhead)	10057	$20.00	
1993	Police Officer	10688	$31.00	Toys 'R' Us
1993	Romantic Bride	1861	$30.00	
1993	Royal Invitation	2969	$125.00	Spiegel
1993	Royal Splendor	10950	$375.00	Porcelain
1993	Secret Hearts	7902	$20.00	
1993	Secret Hearts (black)	3836	$25.00	

Barbie® Dolls

Listed by Year

Year / Doll	Number	Value	Store/Collection
1993 Silken Flame (blonde)	11099	$750.00	Disney
1993 Silver Screen	11652	$150.00	F.A.O. Schwarz
1993 Sparkling Splendor	10994	$45.00	Service Merchandise
1993 Special Black Ponytail Club Outfit	N/A	$500.00	You've Come A Long Way
1993 Special Expressions	10048	$25.00	Woolworth
1993 Special Expressions (black)	N/A	$25.00	Woolworth
1993 Special Expressions (Hispanic)	10050	$25.00	Woolworth
1993 Spots 'n Dots	10491	$30.00	Toys 'R' Us
1993 Super Star	10592	$35.00	Wal-Mart
1993 Super Star (black)	10711	$35.00	Wal-Mart
1993 Talking Perfectly Plaid Set (auburn)	1193	Rtl	Sears
1993 Troll	10257	$15.00	
1993 Twinkle Lights (black)	N/A	$30.00	
1993 Twinkle Lights Pink	N/A	$35.00	
1993 Western Stampin'	10293	$25.00	
1993 Winter Princess	10655	$550.00	Princess Collection
1993 Winter Royal	10658	$95.00	Sam's Wholesale Club
1994 35th Anniversary Curly Bangs (blonde)	N/A	$525.00	Mattel's Barbie Festival
1994 35th Anniversary Curly Bangs (redhead)	N/A	$525.00	Mattel's Barbie Festival
1994 35th Anniversary Nostalgic (blonde)	11589	$25.00	
1994 35th Anniversary Nostalgic (brunette)	11782	$45.00	
1994 Air Force (Thunderbirds)	11552	$75.00	
1994 Astronaut	12149	$35.00	Toys 'R' Us
1994 Astronaut (black)	12150	$45.00	Toys 'R' Us
1994 Bedtime	11079	$15.00	
1994 Bedtime (black)	11184	$15.00	
1994 Bicyclin'	11689	$30.00	
1994 Bicyclin' (black)	11817	$25.00	
1994 Birthday	11333	$25.00	
1994 Birthday (black)	11334	$25.00	
1994 Camp	11074	$12.00	
1994 City Sophisticate	12005	$95.00	Service Merchandise
1994 Country & Western Star	12097	$30.00	Wal-Mart
1994 Country & Western Star (black)	N/A	$30.00	Wal-Mart
1994 Country & Western Star (Hispanic)	N/A	$30.00	Wal-Mart
1994 Cut 'n Style #1 (blonde)	12639	$12.00	
1994 Cut 'n Style #2 (black)	12642	$12.00	
1994 Cut 'n Style (brunette)	12643	$12.00	
1994 Cut 'n Style (redhead)	12644	$12.00	
1994 Dance 'n Twirl	11902	$55.00	

BARBIE® DOLLS

Listed by Year

YEAR / DOLL	NUMBER	VALUE	STORE/COLLECTION
1994 Dance 'n Twirl (black)	12143	$50.00	
1994 Dr. Barbie (black with white baby)	11814	$50.00	Toys 'R' Us
1994 Dr. Barbie (brunette)	11160	$250.00	Mattel Festival Doll
1994 Dr. Barbie (white with black baby)	11160	$50.00	Toys 'R' Us
1994 Dream Dancing	11902	Rtl	
1994 Dream Dancing (black)	12143	Rtl	
1994 Dress 'n Fun	10776	$6.00	
1994 Dress 'n Fun (black)	12143	$6.00	
1994 Dress 'n Fun (Hispanic)	11102	$6.00	
1994 Dutch	11104	$24.00	Dolls of the World Series
1994 Egyptian Queen	11397	$100.00	Great Eras Collection
1994 Emerald Elegance	12322	$40.00	Toys 'R' Us
1994 Emerald Elegance (black)	12323	$30.00	Toys 'R' Us
1994 Evening Extravaganza (pink)	11622	$95.00	Classique Collection
1994 Evening Extravaganza (yellow)	11637	$95.00	Classique Collection
1994 Evening Sensation	1278	$65.00	J.C. Penney
1994 Evergreen Princess	12123	$135.00	Princess Collection
1994 Evergreen Princess (redhead)	13173	$650.00	Walt Disney Convention
1994 Festival Pair (redhead & brunette)	N/A	$1200.00	Mattel Festival Doll
1994 Glitter Hair (black)	11332	$12.00	
1994 Glitter Hair (blonde)	10965	$12.00	
1994 Glitter Hair (burnette)	10966	$12.00	
1994 Glitter Hair (redhead)	10968	$12.00	
1994 Gold Jubilee	12009	$1400.00	Jubilee Series
1994 Gymnast	12127	$14.00	
1994 Gymnast (black)	12153	$14.00	
1994 Gymnast (brunette)	11921	$250.00	Mattel Festival Doll
1994 Happy Holidays	12155	$175.00	Happy Holidays Collection
1994 Happy Holidays	12155	$650.00	Mattel Festival Doll
1994 Happy Holidays (black)	12196	$125.00	Happy Holidays Collection
1994 Holiday Dreams	12192	$35.00	Supermarket
1994 Kenyan	11181	$25.00	Dolls of the World Series
1994 Limited Edition Sale	N/A	$395.00	Mattel Festival Doll
1994 Little Debbie	10123	$75.00	Little Debbie Snack Cakes
1994 Locket Surprise	10963	$14.00	
1994 Locket Surprise (black)	11224	$14.00	
1994 Mattel Special Curley Bangs (brunette)	N/A	$350.00	Mattel Festival Doll
1994 My First Barbie	11294	$10.00	
1994 My First Barbie (Asian)	11342	$10.00	
1994 My First Barbie (black)	11340	$10.00	

Barbie® Dolls

Listed by Year

Year / Doll	Number	Value	Store/Collection
1994 My First Barbie (Hispanic)	11341	$10.00	
1994 My Size	2517	$150.00	
1994 My Size Bride	12052	$175.00	
1994 My Size Bride (black)	12053	$150.00	
1994 Native American #2	11609	$24.00	Dolls of the World Series
1994 Neptune Fantasy face dressed magician	4248	$450.00	Magic of Barbie in Birmingham
1994 Night Dazzle	12191	$65.00	J.C. Penney
1994 Night Dazzle	12191	$650.00	Mattel Festival Doll
1994 Party Time	12243	$23.00	Toys 'R' Us
1994 Pog Barbie	13239	$15.00	Toys 'R' Us
1994 Polly Pockets	12412	$40.00	Hill's
1994 Queen of Hearts	12046	$230.00	Bob Mackie
1994 Rainbow	N/A	$595.00	Mattel Festival Doll
1994 Red Velvet	N/A	$495.00	Mattel Festival Doll
1994 Ruffle Fun	12433	$12.00	
1994 Ruffle Fun (black)	12434	$12.00	
1994 Ruffle Fun (Hispanic)	12435	$12.00	
1994 Savy Shopper	12152	$175.00	Bloomingdale's
1994 Scarlett Green Velvet (1st in series)	12045	$95.00	Hollywood Legends
1994 Season's Greetings	12384	$125.00	Sam's Wholesale Club
1994 Shopping Spree	12749	$25.00	F.A.O. Schwarz
1994 Silken Flame (brunette)	1249	$225.00	Porcelain
1994 Silver Sweetheart	12410	$55.00	Sears
1994 Slumber Party	12696	$14.00	
1994 Slumber Party (black)	12697	$14.00	
1994 Snow Princess	11875	$135.00	Enchanted Season
1994 Snow Princess (brunette)	12905	$1800.00	Mattel Festival Doll
1994 Southern Belle	11478	$95.00	Great Eras Collection
1994 Sun Jewel	10953	$10.00	
1994 Supertalk	N/A	$40.00	
1994 Supertalk (black)	N/A	$40.00	
1994 Swim 'n Dive	11505	$20.00	
1994 Swim 'n Dive (black)	11734	$20.00	
1994 Theatre Elegance	12077	$135.00	Spiegel
1994 Toothfairy	11645	$25.00	Wal-Mart
1994 Treasures	N/A	$65.00	Kraft
1994 Uptown Chic	11623	$75.00	Classique Collection
1994 Valentine	12675	$15.00	Special Edition
1994 Victorian Elegance	12579	$110.00	Hallmark
1994 Wacky Warehouse II	1859	$65.00	Kool Aid

BARBIE® DOLLS

Listed by Store/Collection

STORE/COLLECTION	DOLL	YEAR	NUMBER	VALUE
30th Anniversary	Pink Jubilee	1989	None	$2000.00
American Beauty Collection	Army	1989	3936	$35.00
American Beauty Collection	Mardi Gras	1990	4930	$100.00
American Stories Series	Colonial	1995	12578	$25.00
American Stories Series	Pilgrim	1995	12577	$23.00
American Stories Series	Pioneer	1995	12680	$23.00
Ames	Country Looks	1992	N/A	$25.00
Ames	Denim 'n Lace	1992	2452	$35.00
Ames	Hot Looks	1991	5756	$35.00
Ames	Party in Pink	1991	2909	$35.00
Applause	Barbie Style	1990	5315	$45.00
Applause	Beauty Belle	1991	4553	$25.00
Applause	Holiday Doll	1991	3406	$45.00
Ballet Series	Nutcracker	1992	5472	$250.00
Ballet Series	Swan Lake	1991	1648	$175.00
Barbie Around the World	Japanese International	1985	9481	$300.00
Barbie Convention	Beauty Secrets	1980	1290	$300.00
Barbie Convention	North West Barbie Convention Dolls	1990	None	$350.00
Barbie Deep in the Heart of Texas	My First Ballerina dressed as cowgirl	1990	1280	$300.00
Barbie Doll Reunion	Sun Gold Malibu	1986	1067	$200.00
Barbie Doll's Pow Wow	Fashion Jeans doll with pioneer outfit	1983	5315	$450.00
Barbie in Seattle	Sun Gold Malibu dressed as flower	1988	1067	$300.00
Barbie Loves a Fairytale	Dress Me	1991	5696	$250.00
Barbie Loves New York	Loving You in Red Silver Sensation	1984	7072	$450.00
Barbie Wedding Dreams	Dream Bride Spec. Wedding Gown	1991	1623	$30.00
Ben Franklin	Plus 3	1976	N/A	$75.00
BillyBoy	Feelin' Groovy	1986	3421	$175.00
Bloomingdale's	Bloomingdale's Donna Karan NY (blonde)	1995	14545	$95.00
Bloomingdale's	Bloomingdale's Donna Karan NY (brunette)	1995	14452	$110.00
Bloomingdale's	Savy Shopper	1994	12152	$175.00
Bob Mackie	Empress Bride	1992	4247	$895.00
Bob Mackie	Goddess of the Sun	1995	14056	$225.00
Bob Mackie	Gold	1990	5405	$900.00
Bob Mackie	Masquerade Ball	1993	10803	$350.00
Bob Mackie	Neptune Fantasy	1992	4248	$950.00
Bob Mackie	Platinum	1991	2704	$750.00
Bob Mackie	Queen of Hearts	1994	12046	$230.00
Bob Mackie	Starlight Splender	1991	2703	$750.00
Campus Collection	Ma-Ba	1987	N/A	$65.00
Children's Collector Series	Rapunzel	1995	13016	$40.00

BARBIE® DOLLS

Listed by Store/Collection

STORE/COLLECTION	DOLL	YEAR	NUMBER	VALUE
Children's Palace	Barbie Doll	1990	N/A	$45.00
Children's Palace	Barbie Doll (black)	1990	N/A	$45.00
Children's Palace	Disney Special (with mouse hat)	1991	4385	$50.00
Christmas	Angel Lights	1993	10610	$125.00
Classique Collection	Benefit Ball	1992	1521	$150.00
Classique Collection	City Style	1993	10149	$95.00
Classique Collection	Evening Extravaganza (pink)	1994	11622	$95.00
Classique Collection	Evening Extravaganza (yellow)	1994	11637	$95.00
Classique Collection	Midnight Gala	1995	12999	$60.00
Classique Collection	Opening Night	1993	N/A	$95.00
Classique Collection	Uptown Chic	1994	11623	$75.00
Department Store	Ballerina on Tour	1976	9093	$175.00
Department Store	Beautiful Bride	1976	9599	$300.00
Department Store	Golden Dreams (2nd issue)	1981	3533	$60.00
Department Store	Hawaiian	1975	7470	$50.00
Department Store	Hawaiian #1 (one-piece swimsuit)	1981	7470	$40.00
Department Store	Hawaiian #2 (two-piece swimsuit)	1983	7470	$40.00
Department Store	Kissing (extra dress)	1980	2597	$45.00
Department Store	The Beach Party	1981	1703	$100.00
Department Store	Twirly Curls	1983	5579	30.00
Designer Collection	Christian Dior No. 1	1995	13168	$175.00
Disney	Crystal Rhapsody (brunette)	1992	10201	$750.00
Disney	Disney Character Barbie	1990	9835	$50.00
Disney	Disney Fun	1992	10247	$45.00
Disney	Gay Parisienne (redhead)	1991	9973	$750.00
Disney	Plantation Belle	1992	5351	$750.00
Disney	Silken Flame (blonde)	1993	11099	$750.00
Dolls of the World Series	Australian	1993	7344	$22.00
Dolls of the World Series	Brazilian	1990	9094	$35.00
Dolls of the World Series	Canadian	1988	4928	$75.00
Dolls of the World Series	Chinese	1993	11180	$24.00
Dolls of the World Series	Czechoslovakian	1991	7330	$110.00
Dolls of the World Series	Dolls of the World Set	1995	13939	$75.00
Dolls of the World Series	Dutch	1994	11104	$24.00
Dolls of the World Series	English	1992	4973	$50.00
Dolls of the World Series	Eskimo	1983	3898	$120.00
Dolls of the World Series	Eskimo	1991	9844	$55.00
Dolls of the World Series	German	1987	3188	$110.00
Dolls of the World Series	German	1995	12698	$24.00
Dolls of the World Series	Greek	1986	2997	$85.00

In 1994 Bloomingdale's decided to offer an exclusive Barbie doll. Pictured here is Savvy Shopper Barbie. This doll was designed by Nichole Miller. I think the most interesting thing about this doll is the print on her silk coat. Ms. Miller designed it especially for Barbie. Notice Barbie doll's name and initial on the print. The print also contains various cosmetic articles.

Barbie, Queen of the Nile? This doll was issued in 1994. Her name is Egyptian Queen. She is the fourth entry in the Great Eras series. This doll wears gold-tone sandals.

FAMILY & FRIENDS DOLLS

Listed Alphabetically

ITEM	YEAR	NUMBERS	VALUE	DOLL
Talking Christie	1968	1126	$150.00	Christie
Talking Christie (darker skin)	1971	1126	$150.00	Christie
Talking Christie (new window box)	1969	1126	$150.00	Christie
Talking Julia	1969	1128	$150.00	Julia
Talking Julia (darker skin)	1971	1128	$150.00	Julia
Talking Ken	1969	1111	$100.00	Ken
Talking Ken (Baggie, non-talking)	1973	1111	$20.00	Ken
Talking P.J.	1969	1113	$155.00	P.J.
Talking P.J. (Baggie, non-talking)	1973	1113	$20.00	P.J.
Talking Stacey	1968	1125	$290.00	Stacey
Talking Stacey (blue/silver suite)	1970	1125	$365.00	Stacey
Talking Stacey (new window box)	1969	1125	$350.00	Stacey
Talking Truly Scrumptious	1969	1107	$350.00	Truly
Teen Dance Jazzie	1988	3634	$25.00	Jazzie
Teen Sweetheart Skipper	1988	4855	N/A	Skipper
Teentime Courtney	1989	1952	$25.00	Courtney
Teentime Skipper	1989	1951	N/A	Skipper
The Beat Christie	1990	2752	$25.00	Christie
The Beat Midge	1990	2754	$25.00	Midge
The Sensations Becky	1988	4977	$25.00	Becky
The Sensations Belinda	1988	4976	$25.00	Belinda
The Sensations Bopsy	1988	4967	$25.00	Bopsy
Todd Doll	1966	3580	$160.00	Todd
Todd Doll (Titian)	1967	3590	$65.00	Todd
Todd (reissue, Europe)	1967	Foreign	$25.00	Todd
Toontown Stacie	1993	11587	$35.00	Stacie
Totally Hair Courtney	1991	N/A	$30.00	Courtney
Totally Hair Ken	1992	1115	$30.00	Ken
Totally Hair Whitney	1992	7735	$45.00	Whitney
Tracy Doll (Bridal)	1983	4103	$40.00	Tracy
Trade-In Special Living Skipper	1970	1147	$125.00	Skipper
Tropical Ken	1986	1020	$12.00	Ken
Tropical Ken (black)	1986	1023	$15.00	Ken
Tropical Miko	1986	2056	$20.00	Miko
Tropical Skipper	1986	1021	$20.00	Skipper
Tropical Splash Christie	1995	12451	$5.00	Christie
Tropical Splash Ken	1995	12447	$5.00	Ken
Tropical Splash Kira	1995	12449	$5.00	Kira
Tropical Splash Skipper	1995	12448	$5.00	Skipper
Tropical Splash Steven	1995	12452	$5.00	Steven

FAMILY & FRIENDS DOLLS

Listed Alphabetically

ITEM	YEAR	NUMBERS	VALUE	DOLL
Tropical Splash Teresa	1995	12450	$5.00	Teresa
Truly Scrumptious (Straight Leg)	1969	1108	$400.00	Truly
Tutti and Todd Sundae Treat Play Set	1966	3556	$275.00	Todd
Tutti Doll (blonde)	1966	3350	$75.00	Tutti
Tutti Doll (brunette)	1966	3350	$75.00	Tutti
Tutti Doll (different dress, brunette)	1967	3550	$40.00	Tutti
Tutti Doll (different dress, brunette)	1967	3580	$40.00	Tutti
Tutti (reissue, Europe)	1967	Foreign	$25.00	Tutti
Twiggy Doll	1967	1185	$350.00	Twiggy
Twist 'n Turn Casey (blonde)	1969	1180	$300.00	Casey
Twist 'n Turn Casey (brunette)	1969	1180	$300.00	Casey
Twist 'n Turn Christie	1970	1119	$150.00	Christie
Twist 'n Turn Francie	1969	1170	$325.00	Francie
Twist 'n Turn Francie (black)	1967	1100	$985.00	Francie
Twist 'n Turn Francie (blonde)	1967	1170	$75.00	Francie
Twist 'n Turn Francie (brunette)	1967	1170	$75.00	Francie
Twist 'n Turn Francie (no bangs, blonde)	1971	1170	$500.00	Francie
Twist 'n Turn Francie (no bangs, brunette)	1971	1170	$500.00	Francie
Twist 'n Turn Julia	1969	1127	$150.00	Julia
Twist 'n Turn P.J.	1970	1118	$100.00	P.J.
Twist 'n Turn Skipper	1970	1105	$100.00	Skipper
Twist 'n Turn Skipper (new 2 curl hairstyle)	1969	1105	$100.00	Skipper
Twist 'n Turn Stacey (aqua/rose suit)	1970	1165	$332.00	Stacey
Twist 'n Turn Stacey (blonde)	1969	1165	$298.00	Stacey
Twist 'n Turn Stacey (brunette, new box)	1969	1165	$295.00	Stacey
Twist 'n Turn Stacey (Titian)	1968	1165	$300.00	Stacey
Walk Lively Ken	1972	1184	$80.00	Ken
Walk Lively Miss America	1972	3200	$75.00	Miss America
Walk Lively Steffie	1972	1183	$150.00	Steffie
Walking Jamie	1970	1132	$250.00	Jamie
Walking Jamie Strollin' In Style	1972	1247	$450.00	Jamie
Walking My Dolly	1966	3552	$150.00	Tutti
Walking My Dolly (Europe)	1975	7454	$100.00	Tutti
Wedding Day Alan	1991	9607	$20.00	Alan
Wedding Day Kelly & Todd	1991	2820	$35.00	Kelly
Wedding Day Ken	1991	9609	$20.00	Ken
Wedding Day Midge	1991	9606	$20.00	Midge
Western Fun Ken	1990	9934	$20.00	Ken
Western Fun Nia	1990	9933	$20.00	Nia
Western Ken	1982	3600	$30.00	Ken

FAMILY & FRIENDS DOLLS

Listed Alphabetically

Item	Year	Numbers	Value	Doll
Western Skipper	1982	5029	$30.00	Skipper
Western Stampin' Ken	1993	10294	$25.00	Ken
Western Stampin' Tara Lynn	1993	10295	$25.00	Tara
Wet 'n Wild Christie	1990	4121	$20.00	Christie
Wet 'n Wild Ken	1990	4104	$20.00	Ken
Wet 'n Wild Kira	1990	4120	$20.00	Kira
Wet 'n Wild Skipper	1990	4138	$20.00	Skipper
Wet 'n Wild Steven	1990	4137	$20.00	Steven
Wet 'n Wild Teresa	1990	4136	$20.00	Teresa
Wet 'n Wild Whitney	1990	4136	$80.00	Whitney
Wig Wardrobe Molded	1965	1009	$225.00	Midge
Workout Jazzie	1988	3633	N/A	Jazzie
Workout Teen Doll	1988	5899	N/A	Skipper
Yellowstone Kelley	1974	7808	$200.00	Kelley

FAMILY & FRIENDS

Listed by Doll

DOLL	ITEM	YEAR	NUMBER	VALUE
Alan	Wedding Day Alan	1991	9607	$20.00
Allan	Allan (Bendable Leg)	1965	1010	$300.00
Allan	Allan Straight Legs (redhead)	1964	1000	$98.00
Angie	Pretty Pairs Angie 'n Tangie	1970	1135	$255.00
Becky	The Sensations Becky	1988	4977	$25.00
Belinda	The Sensations Belinda	1988	4976	$25.00
Bopsy	The Sensations Bopsy	1988	4967	$25.00
Brad	Brad Doll (Bendable Leg)	1970	1142	$150.00
Brad	Brad Doll (Bendable Leg, darker skin)	1971	1142	$135.00
Brad	Talking Brad	1970	1114	$125.00
Brad	Talking Brad (darker skin)	1971	1114	$125.00
Buffy	Buffy and Mrs. Beasley	1968	3357	$175.00
Cara	Ballerina Cara	1976	9528	$60.00
Cara	Deluxe Quick Curl Cara	1976	9220	$60.00
Cara	Free Moving Cara	1975	7283	$30.00
Cara	Quick Curl Cara	1975	7291	$35.00
Cara	Quick Curl Cara (Canada)	1973	Foreign	$50.00
Carla	Carla	1976	7377	$150.00
Carla	Carla (Europe)	1976	7377	$45.00
Carla	Carla (reissue Europe)	1976	7377	$50.00
Casey	Casey Doll (Baggie)	1975	9000	$40.00
Casey	Casey Doll (blonde)	1967	1180	$300.00
Casey	Casey Doll (brunette)	1967	1180	$300.00
Casey	Twist 'n Turn Casey (blonde)	1969	1180	$300.00
Casey	Twist 'n Turn Casey (brunette)	1969	1180	$300.00
Chelsie	High School Chelsie	1988	3698	$40.00
Chris	Chris Doll (blond)	1967	3570	$75.00
Chris	Chris Doll (brunet)	1967	3570	$150.00
Chris	Chris (reissue Europe)	1974	81300	$75.00
Christie	All American Christie	1991	9425	$25.00
Christie	Barbie and the All Stars Christie	1990	9352	$25.00
Christie	Beach Blast Christie	1989	3253	$25.00
Christie	Beauty Secrets Christie	1980	1295	$45.00
Christie	Benetton Christie	1992	9407	$35.00
Christie	Benetton Shopping Christie	1992	4887	$50.00
Christie	California Dream Christie	1988	4443	$25.00
Christie	Cool Times Christie	1989	3217	$20.00
Christie	Fashion Photo Christie	1978	N/A	$60.00
Christie	Glitter Beach Christie	1993	4907	$25.00
Christie	Golden Dream Christie	1981	3249	$50.00

Family & Friends Dolls

Listed by Doll

Doll	Item	Year	Number	Value
Christie	Hawaiian Fun Christie	1991	5944	$10.00
Christie	Island Fun Christie	1988	4093	$25.00
Christie	Kissing Christie	1980	2955	$50.00
Christie	Lights 'n Lace Christie	1991	9728	$25.00
Christie	Live Action Christie	1971	1175	$150.00
Christie	Malibu Christie	1975	7745	$35.00
Christie	Malibu Christie (new box)	1975	7745	$35.00
Christie	Malibu Christie (new rose box)	1976	7745	$75.00
Christie	Malibue Christie	1978	7745	$30.00
Christie	Pink and Pretty Christie	1982	3555	$40.00
Christie	Pink & Pretty Christie	1981	3554	$45.00
Christie	Pretty Reflections Christie	1979	1295	$85.00
Christie	Rappin' Rockin' Christie	1992	3265	$25.00
Christie	Rollerblade Christie	1992	2217	$30.00
Christie	Style Magic Christie	1989	1290	$25.00
Christie	Sun Lovin' Malibu Christie	1980	7745	$30.00
Christie	Sun Sensation Christie	1992	1393	$15.00
Christie	Sunsational Malibu Christie	1981	7745	$20.00
Christie	Sunsational Malibu Christie	1982	7745	$30.00
Christie	Super Star Christie	1976	N/A	$80.00
Christie	Talking Christie	1968	1126	$150.00
Christie	Talking Christie (darker skin)	1971	1126	$150.00
Christie	Talking Christie (new window box)	1969	1126	$150.00
Christie	The Beat Christie	1990	2752	$25.00
Christie	Tropical Splash Christie	1995	12451	$5.00
Christie	Twist 'n Turn Christie	1970	1119	$150.00
Christie	Wet 'n Wild Christie	1990	4121	$20.00
Courtney	Baby Sitter Courtney	1991	9434	$10.00
Courtney	Cheerleading Courtney	1993	3933	$10.00
Courtney	Cool Crimp Courtney	1994	11548	$10.00
Courtney	Cool Tops Courtney	1990	7079	$20.00
Courtney	Pet Pals Courtney	1992	2701	$20.00
Courtney	Pizza Party Courtney	1995	12943	$10.00
Courtney	Teentime Courtney	1989	1952	$25.00
Courtney	Totally Hair Courtney	1991	N/A	$30.00
Curtis	Free Moving Curtis	1975	7282	$50.00
Dana	Rocker Dana	1986	1196	$30.00
Dana	Rocker Dana (revised)	1987	3158	$30.00
Dana	Rocker Dancin' Action Dana	1986	3158	$35.00
Dee Dee	Rocker Dancin' Action Dee Dee	1986	3160	$35.00

FAMILY & FRIENDS

Listed by Doll

DOLL	ITEM	YEAR	NUMBER	VALUE
Dee Dee	Rocker Dee Dee	1986	3160	$30.00
Dee Dee	Rocker Dee Dee (revised)	1987	3160	$30.00
Derek	Rocker Derek	1986	2428	$30.00
Derek	Rocker Derek (revised)	1987	3137	$30.00
Derek	Rocker Hot Rockin' Derek	1986	3173	$35.00
Devon	Dance Club Devon	1989	3513	$35.00
Diva	Rocker Dancin' Action Diva	1986	3159	$35.00
Diva	Rocker Diva	1986	2427	$30.00
Diva	Rocker Diva (revised)	1987	3159	$30.00
Dude	High School Dude	1988	3637	$40.00
Fluff	Living Fluff	1971	1143	$175.00
Francie	Busy Francie with Holdin' Hands	1972	3313	$300.00
Francie	Francie Doll 1st issue (black, red oxidized)	1967	1100	$900.00
Francie	Francie Doll 2nd issue (black, dark brown)	1967	1100	$800.00
Francie	Francie Doll 2nd issue (blonde)	1966	1130	N/A
Francie	Francie Doll 2nd issue (brunette)	1966	1130	N/A
Francie	Francie Doll (Baggie)	1975	7699	$40.00
Francie	Francie Doll (Bendable Leg)	1966	1130	$250.00
Francie	Francie Doll (Straight Legs blonde)	1966	1140	$300.00
Francie	Francie Doll (Straight Legs brunette)	1966	1140	$175.00
Francie	Francie (Germany)	1971	Foreign	N/A
Francie	Growin' Pretty Hair (extra hair pieces)	1971	1074	$175.00
Francie	Growin' Pretty Hair Francie	1970	1129	$200.00
Francie	Hair Happenin's Francie	1970	1122	$250.00
Francie	Malibu Francie	1973	1068	$45.00
Francie	Malibu Francie	1978	1068	$30.00
Francie	Malibu Francie (new box)	1975	1068	$40.00
Francie	Malibu Francie (new rose box)	1976	1068	$40.00
Francie	Malibu Francie (The Sun Set)	1971	1068	$30.00
Francie	Quick Curl Francie	1973	4222	$75.00
Francie	Rise 'n Shine	1971	1194	N/A
Francie	Twist 'n Turn Francie	1969	1170	$325.00
Francie	Twist 'n Turn Francie (black)	1967	1100	$985.00
Francie	Twist 'n Turn Francie (blonde)	1967	1170	$75.00
Francie	Twist 'n Turn Francie (brunette)	1967	1170	$75.00
Francie	Twist 'n Turn Francie (no bangs, blonde)	1971	1170	$500.00
Francie	Twist 'n Turn Francie (no bangs, brunette)	1971	1170	$500.00
Ginger	Growing U p Ginger	1976	9222	$60.00
Jamie	Walking Jamie	1970	1132	$250.00
Jamie	Walking Jamie Strollin' In Style	1972	1247	$450.00

FAMILY & FRIENDS DOLLS

Listed by Doll

DOLL	ITEM	YEAR	NUMBER	VALUE
Janet	Happy Meal Janet	1994	11477	$14.00
Janet	Polly Pockets Janet	1995	12984	$10.00
Jazzie	Cheerleader Jazzie	1988	3631	$25.00
Jazzie	Glitter Beach Jazzie	1993	4935	$5.00
Jazzie	Hawaiian Fun Jazzie	1991	9294	$10.00
Jazzie	High School Jazzie	1988	3635	$25.00
Jazzie	Sun Lovin' Malibu Jazzie	1990	4088	$20.00
Jazzie	Sun Sensation Jazzie	1992	5473	$15.00
Jazzie	Swim Suit Jazzie	1988	3632	$25.00
Jazzie	Teen Dance Jazzie	1988	3634	$25.00
Jazzie	Workout Jazzie	1988	3633	N/A
Julia	Talking Julia	1969	1128	$150.00
Julia	Talking Julia (darker skin)	1971	1128	$150.00
Julia	Twist 'n Turn Julia	1969	1127	$150.00
Kayla	Dance Club Kayla	1989	3512	$35.00
Kayla	Locket Surprise Kayla	1994	11209	$14.00
Kelley	Quick Curl Kelley	1973	4221	$80.00
Kelley	Yellowstone Kelley	1974	7808	$200.00
Kelly	Baby Sister Kelly	1995	12489	$10.00
Kelly	Baby Sister Kelly (black)	1995	13256	$10.00
Kelly	Barbie Doll Strolling Set	1995	13742	$15.00
Kelly	Barbie Doll Strolling Set (black)	1995	13743	$15.00
Kelly	Wedding Day Kelly & Todd	1991	2820	$35.00
Ken	30th Anniversary Ken	1991	11581	$225.00
Ken	Air Force Ken	1994	11554	$25.00
Ken	Air Force Ken (black)	1994	11555	$25.00
Ken	All American Ken	1991	9424	$25.00
Ken	All Star Ken	1982	3553	$25.00
Ken	All Star Ken	1990	9361	$20.00
Ken	Animal Lovin' Ken	1989	1351	$35.00
Ken	Army Ken	1993	N/A	$20.00
Ken	Army Ken (black)	1993	5619	$20.00
Ken	Baywatch Ken	1995	13200	$15.00
Ken	Baywatch Ken (black)	1995	13259	$15.00
Ken	Beach Blast Ken	1989	3238	$15.00
Ken	Beach Time Ken	1984	9103	$35.00
Ken	Bendable Leg Ken Gift Set	1970	1436	N/A
Ken	Benetton Ken	1991	9406	$50.00
Ken	Benetton Shopping Ken	1992	4876	$50.00
Ken	Busy Ken	1972	3314	$150.00

Family & Friends

Listed by Doll

Doll	Item	Year	Number	Value
Ken	California Dream Ken	1988	4441	$20.00
Ken	Camp Ken	1994	10075	$15.00
Ken	Cool Times Ken	1989	3215	$20.00
Ken	Costume Ball Ken	1991	7154	$25.00
Ken	Costume Ball Ken (black)	1991	7160	$25.00
Ken	Crystal Ken	1984	4898	$25.00
Ken	Crystal Ken (black)	1984	9036	$35.00
Ken	Dance Club Ken	1989	3511	$35.00
Ken	Dance Magic Ken	1990	7081	$25.00
Ken	Dance Magic Ken (black)	1990	7082	$25.00
Ken	Day-To-Night Ken	1985	9019	$15.00
Ken	Day-To-Night Ken (black)	1985	9018	$15.00
Ken	Doctor Ken	1987	4118	$25.00
Ken	Dr. Ken	1987	4118	$25.00
Ken	Dream Date Ken	1983	4077	$30.00
Ken	Dream Glow Ken	1986	2250	$25.00
Ken	Dream Glow Ken (black)	1986	2421	$25.00
Ken	Earring Magic Ken	1993	2290	$25.00
Ken	Fashion Jeans Ken	1982	5316	$50.00
Ken	Flight Time Ken	1990	9600	$40.00
Ken	Free Moving Ken	1975	7280	$50.00
Ken	Funtime Ken	1975	7194	$25.00
Ken	Funtime Ken (Germany)	1975	7194	N/A
Ken	Glitter Beach Ken	1993	4904	$5.00
Ken	Gold Medal Skier Ken	1975	7261	$75.00
Ken	Golden Night Ken (Canada)	1980	Foreign	$35.00
Ken	Great Shape Ken	1984	7318	$25.00
Ken	Hawaiian Fun Ken	1991	5941	$10.00
Ken	Hawaiian Ken	1981	2960	$50.00
Ken	Hawaiian Ken	1983	7495	$40.00
Ken	Hollywood Hair Ken	1993	4829	$23.00
Ken	Horse Lovin' Ken	1983	3600	$45.00
Ken	Hot Skatin' Ken	1995	13513	$10.00
Ken	Ice Capades Ken	1990	7375	$25.00
Ken	Island Fun Ken	1988	4060	$35.00
Ken	Jewel Secrets Ken	1987	1719	$25.00
Ken	Jewel Secrets Ken (black)	1987	3232	$25.00
Ken	Jogging Ken (Canada)	1981	Foreign	$30.00
Ken	Ken (Baggie, Talking Body-Live Action Head)	1974	1159	$45.00
Ken	Ken Doll	1964	0750	N/A

FAMILY & FRIENDS DOLLS

Listed by Doll

DOLL	ITEM	YEAR	NUMBER	VALUE
Ken	Ken Doll (1st issue, flocked, Straight Leg)	1961	750	$200.00
Ken	Ken Doll (Bendable Leg)	1965	1020	300.00
Ken	Ken Doll (Bendable Leg)	1969	1020	$100.00
Ken	Ken Doll (Bendable Leg)	1970	1124	$100.00
Ken	Ken Doll (Bendable Leg, painted cheeks)	1965	1020	N/A
Ken	Ken Doll (blond)	1961	750	N/A
Ken	Ken Doll (brown)	1961	750	N/A
Ken	Ken Doll (brunet)	1961	750	N/A
Ken	Ken Doll (crew cut, blond)	1963	750	N/A
Ken	Ken Doll (crew cut, brunet)	1963	750	N/A
Ken	Ken Doll (painted brunet hair)	1962	750	N/A
Ken	Ken Doll (Straight Leg, flocked)	1961	950	$200.00
Ken	Ken Doll (Straight Leg, flocked brunet)	1961	750	$180.00
Ken	Ken (Straight Leg, molded hair, ¼ shorter)	1963	750	$140.00
Ken	Ken (Straight Leg, molded hair painted blond)	1962	750	$95.00
Ken	Live Action Ken	1971	1159	$100.00
Ken	Live Action Ken (Baggie)	1973	1159	$27.00
Ken	Live Action on Stage Ken	1971	1172	$150.00
Ken	Locket Surprise Ken	1994	10964	$14.00
Ken	Malibu Ken (darker skin, new box)	1976	1088	$50.00
Ken	Malibu Ken (new box)	1975	1088	$50.00
Ken	Malibu Ken (new rose box)	1976	1088	$50.00
Ken	Malibu Ken Surf's Up	1971	1248	$30.00
Ken	Malibu Ken (The Sun Set)	1971	1088	$30.00
Ken	Marine Ken	1991	7574	$25.00
Ken	Marine Ken (black)	1992	7594	$25.00
Ken	Mod Hair Ken	1973	4224	$65.00
Ken	Mod Hair Ken	1974	4234	$45.00
Ken	Motorcycle Ken	1994	12000	Rtl
Ken	Motorcycle Ken (black)	1994	12126	$5.00
Ken	Music Lovin' Ken	1985	2388	$45.00
Ken	My First Ken	1989	1389	$15.00
Ken	My First Ken	1990	9940	$15.00
Ken	My First Ken	1991	9940	$15.00
Ken	My First Ken	1992	3841	$15.00
Ken	My First Ken	1993	1503	Rtl
Ken	My First Ken (black)	1993	3876	Rtl
Ken	Now Look Ken (longer hair)	1976	9342	$45.00
Ken	Now Look Ken (shorter hair)	1976	9342	$65.00
Ken	Perfume Giving Ken	1988	4554	N/A

FAMILY & FRIENDS

Listed by Doll

DOLL	ITEM	YEAR	NUMBER	VALUE
Ken	Perfume Giving Ken (black)	1988	4555	N/A
Ken	Perfume Pretty Ken	1987	4554	$30.00
Ken	Perfume Pretty Ken (black)	1987	4555	$30.00
Ken	Rappin' Rockin' Ken	1992	4903	$25.00
Ken	Rocker Hot Rockin' Ken	1986	3131	$35.00
Ken	Rocker Ken	1986	3131	$30.00
Ken	Rocker Ken (revised)	1987	3131	$30.00
Ken	Roller Skating Ken	1981	1881	$50.00
Ken	Rollerblade Ken	1992	2215	$30.00
Ken	Secret Heart Ken	1993	7988	$20.00
Ken	Shaving Fun Ken	1995	12956	$10.00
Ken	Ski Fun Ken	1992	7512	$20.00
Ken	Spanish Talking Ken	1970	8372	$200.00
Ken	Sparkle Eyes Ken	1992	3149	$25.00
Ken	Sparkle Surprise Ken	1992	3149	N/A
Ken	Sport & Shave Ken	1980	1294	$30.00
Ken	Sports Star Ken (Canada)	1979	Foreign	$40.00
Ken	Sun Charm Ken	1989	9934	$25.00
Ken	Sun Gold Malibu Ken	1984	1088	$20.00
Ken	Sun Gold Malibu Ken (black)	1985	3849	$20.00
Ken	Sun Gold Malibu Ken (Hispanic)	1984	4971	$20.00
Ken	Sun Lovin' Malibu Ken	1979	1088	$30.00
Ken	Sun Sensation Ken	1992	1392	$15.00
Ken	Sun Valley Ken	1974	7809	$125.00
Ken	Sunsational Malibu Ken	1981	1088	$15.00
Ken	Sunsational Malibu Ken	1982	1088	$30.00
Ken	Sunsational Malibu Ken (black)	1982	3849	$30.00
Ken	Sunsational Malibu Ken (Hispanic)	1983	4971	$40.00
Ken	Sunsational Malibu Ken with Hair	1981	3849	$40.00
Ken	Super Sport Ken	1982	5839	$25.00
Ken	Super Star Ken with Free Gift	1977	N/A	$72.00
Ken	Super Star Ken with Ring (1st issue)	1976	N/A	$75.00
Ken	Superstar Ken	1989	1535	$35.00
Ken	Superstar Ken (black)	1989	1550	$35.00
Ken	Talking Busy Ken	1973	1111	$20.00
Ken	Talking Ken	1969	1111	$100.00
Ken	Talking Ken (Baggie, non-talking)	1972	1196	$200.00
Ken	Totally Hair Ken	1992	1115	$30.00
Ken	Tropical Ken	1986	1020	$12.00
Ken	Tropical Ken (black)	1986	1023	$15.00

FAMILY & FRIENDS DOLLS

Listed by Doll

DOLL	ITEM	YEAR	NUMBER	VALUE
Ken	Tropical Splash Ken	1995	12447	$5.00
Ken	Walk Lively Ken	1972	1184	$80.00
Ken	Wedding Day Ken	1991	9609	$20.00
Ken	Western Fun Ken	1990	9934	$20.00
Ken	Western Ken	1982	3600	$30.00
Ken	Western Stampin' Ken	1993	10294	$25.00
Ken	Wet 'n Wild Ken	1990	4104	$20.00
Kevin	Baby Sitter Kevin	1991	9324	$10.00
Kevin	Basketball Kevin	1993	4713	$10.00
Kevin	Cool Crimp Kevin	1994	11549	$10.00
Kevin	Cool Tops Kevin	1990	9351	$20.00
Kevin	Dream Date Kevin	1990	9351	$25.00
Kevin	Pet Pals Kevin	1992	2711	$20.00
Kevin	Pizza Party Kevin	1995	12944	$10.00
Kira	All American Kira	1991	9427	$25.00
Kira	Benetton Kira	1991	9409	$25.00
Kira	Flying Hero Kira	1995	14032	$15.00
Kira	Glitter Beach Kira	1993	4924	$5.00
Kira	Hawaiian Fun Kira	1991	5943	$10.00
Kira	Rollerblade Kira	1992	2218	$30.00
Kira	Sun Jewel Kira	1994	19056	$8.00
Kira	Sun Sensation Kira	1992	1447	$15.00
Kira	Tropical Splash Kira	1995	12449	$5.00
Kira	Wet 'n Wild Kira	1990	4120	$20.00
Lori	Pretty Pairs Lori 'n Rori	1970	1133	$200.00
Marina	Benetton Shopping Marina	1992	4898	$50.00
Midge	All Stars Midge	1990	9360	$20.00
Midge	Bendable Leg Midge	1965	1080	$350.00
Midge	California Dream Midge	1988	4442	$20.00
Midge	Camp Midge	1994	11077	$15.00
Midge	Cool Times Midge	1989	3216	$20.00
Midge	Earring Magic Midge	1993	10256	$25.00
Midge	Midge Doll (Bendable Leg)	1965	860	$500.00
Midge	Midge Doll (Bendable Leg, brunette)	1965	1080	$550.00
Midge	Midge Doll (brunette)	1963	860	N/A
Midge	Midge Doll (no freckles)	1963	860	$400.00
Midge	Midge Doll (Straight Leg, brunette)	1963	860	$125.00
Midge	Midge Doll (Straight Leg with teeth, blonde)	1963	860	$125.00
Midge	Midge Doll (sunny blonde)	1963	860	N/A
Midge	Midge Doll (Titian)	1963	860	N/A

DOLL	ITEM	YEAR	NUMBER	VALUE
Midge	Midge Wedding Party (six doll set)	1991	9852	$125.00
Midge	Ski Fun Midge	1992	7513	$50.00
Midge	Slumber Party Midge	1995	13236	$10.00
Midge	The Beat Midge	1990	2754	$25.00
Midge	Wedding Day Midge	1991	9606	$20.00
Midge	Wig Wardrobe Molded	1965	1009	$225.00
Miko	Beach Blast Miko	1989	3244	$15.00
Miko	Island Fun Miko	1988	4065	$25.00
Miko	Tropical Miko	1986	2056	$20.00
Miss America	Quick Curl Miss America	1976	8697	$75.00
Miss America	Quick Curl Miss America (blonde)	1973	8697	$55.00
Miss America	Quick Curl Miss America (blonde)	1974	8697	N/A
Miss America	Quick Curl Miss America (brunette)	1973	8697	$210.00
Miss America	Quick Curl Miss America (Canada)	1973	8697	$90.00
Miss America	Walk Lively Miss America	1972	3200	$75.00
Nan	Pretty Pairs Nan 'n Fran	1970	1134	$200.00
Nia	Western Fun Nia	1990	9933	$20.00
Nikki	Animal Lovin' Nikki	1989	1352	$35.00
P.J.	Barbie & Friends P.J.	1983	4431	$40.00
P.J.	Deluxe Quick Curl P.J.	1976	9218	$60.00
P.J.	Dream Date P.J.	1983	5869	$30.00
P.J.	Fashion Photo P.J.	1978	2323	$60.00
P.J.	Free Moving P.J.	1975	7281	$50.00
P.J.	Gold Medal Gymnast P.J.	1975	7263	$85.00
P.J.	Gymnast P.J.	1974	7263	$75.00
P.J.	Live Action on Stage P.J.	1971	1153	$215.00
P.J.	Live Action P.J.	1971	1156	$100.00
P.J.	Live Action P.J. (Baggie)	1973	1156	$36.00
P.J.	Malibu P.J. (Baggie)	1973	1187	$20.00
P.J.	Malibu P.J. (new box)	1975	1187	$70.00
P.J.	Malibu P.J. (new rose box)	1976	7281	$75.00
P.J.	Malibu P.J. (The Sun Set)	1971	1187	$30.00
P.J.	New 'n Groovy Talking P.J.	1969	N/A	$150.00
P.J.	Sun Gold Malibu P.J.	1984	1187	$20.00
P.J.	Sun Lovin' Malibu P.J.	1980	1187	$30.00
P.J.	Sunsational Malibu P.J.	1981	1187	$25.00
P.J.	Sunsational Malibu P.J.	1982	1187	$30.00
P.J.	Sweet Roses P.J.	1984	7455	$45.00
P.J.	Talking P.J.	1969	1113	$155.00
P.J.	Talking P.J. (Baggie, non-talking)	1973	1113	$20.00

FAMILY & FRIENDS DOLLS

Listed by Doll

Doll	Item	Year	Number	Value
P.J.	Twist 'n Turn P.J.	1970	1118	$100.00
Ricky	Ricky (redhead)	1965	1090	$150.00
Scott	Scott Doll	1990	1019	$45.00
Scott	Super Teen Scott	1979	1019	$50.00
Shani	Dr. Shani Doll	1994	11814	$18.00
Shani	Sun Jewel Shani	1994	19058	$8.00
Skipper	30th Anniversary Skipper	1994	11396	$200.00
Skipper	Baby Sitter Skipper	1991	9433	$10.00
Skipper	Baby Sitter Skipper	1993	12071	$14.00
Skipper	Baby Sitter Skipper (black)	1991	1599	$14.00
Skipper	Bathtime Fun Skipper	1992	7970	$25.00
Skipper	Baton Twirling Skipper	1993	3931	$10.00
Skipper	Beach Blast Skipper	1989	3242	$15.00
Skipper	Beauty Pageant Skipper	1991	9324	$35.00
Skipper	Camp Skipper	1994	11076	$15.00
Skipper	Cheerleader Teen Skipper	1988	5893	$25.00
Skipper	Cool Crimp Skipper	1994	11179	$10.00
Skipper	Cool Crimp Skipper (black)	1994	11547	$10.00
Skipper	Cool Tops Skipper	1990	4989	$20.00
Skipper	Cool Tops Skipper (black)	1990	5441	$10.00
Skipper	Deluxe Quick Curl Skipper	1975	9428	$65.00
Skipper	Deluxe Quick Curl Skipper (Europe)	1976	9428	$60.00
Skipper	Dream Date Skipper	1990	4817	$30.00
Skipper	Dream Date Skipper (black)	1990	4849	$30.00
Skipper	Funtime Skipper	1975	7193	N/A
Skipper	Funtime Skipper (Germany)	1975	7193	N/A
Skipper	Glitter Beach Skipper	1993	4920	$5.00
Skipper	Great Shape Skipper	1984	7414	$30.00
Skipper	Growing Up Skipper (long pale blonde)	1975	7259	$60.00
Skipper	Growing Up Skipper (short golden blonde)	1975	7259	$65.00
Skipper	Hawaiian Fun Skipper	1991	5942	$10.00
Skipper	Hollywood Hair Skipper	1993	2309	Rtl
Skipper	Homecoming Queen Skipper	1989	1950	$45.00
Skipper	Homecoming Queen Skipper (black)	1989	2390	$45.00
Skipper	Horse Lovin' Skipper	1983	5029	$45.00
Skipper	Hot Stuff Skipper	1985	7927	$15.00
Skipper	Island Fun Skipper	1988	4064	$25.00
Skipper	Jewel Secrets Skipper	1987	3133	$25.00
Skipper	Living Skipper (blonde)	1970	1153	$85.00
Skipper	Living Skipper (new clothes)	1971	1117	$80.00

FAMILY & FRIENDS

Listed by Doll

DOLL	ITEM	YEAR	NUMBER	VALUE
Teresa	Benetton Teresa	1991	9408	$50.00
Teresa	California Dream Teresa	1988	5503	$20.00
Teresa	Camp Teresa	1994	11078	$15.00
Teresa	Cool Times Teresa	1989	3218	$20.00
Teresa	Country Star Teresa	1994	N/A	$25.00
Teresa	Dance Moves Teresa	1995	13084	$15.00
Teresa	Flying Hero Teresa	1995	14031	$15.00
Teresa	Glitter Beach Teresa	1993	4921	$5.00
Teresa	Hollywood Hair Teresa	1993	2316	Rtl
Teresa	Island Fun Teresa	1988	4117	$25.00
Teresa	Lights 'n Lace Teresa	1991	9727	$25.00
Teresa	Quinceanera Teresa	1995	11928	$20.00
Teresa	Party Time Teresa	1994	12244	$15.00
Teresa	Rappin' Rockin' Teresa	1992	3270	$25.00
Teresa	Rollerblade Teresa	1992	2216	$30.00
Teresa	Slumber Party Teresa	1995	13235	$10.00
Teresa	Sun Jewel Teresa	1994	19057	$8.00
Teresa	Sunflower Teresa	1995	13489	$10.00
Teresa	Tropical Splash Teresa	1995	12450	$5.00
Teresa	Wet 'n Wild Teresa	1990	4136	$20.00
Tiff	Pose 'n Play Tiff	1972	1199	$300.00
Todd	Handsome Groom Todd	1983	4253	$40.00
Todd	Happy Meal Todd	1994	11475	$14.00
Todd	Party 'n Play Todd	1993	7903	Rtl
Todd	Todd Doll	1966	3580	$160.00
Todd	Todd Doll (Titian)	1967	3590	$65.00
Todd	Todd (reissue, Europe)	1967	Foreign	$25.00
Todd	Tutti and Todd Sundae Treat Play Set	1966	3556	$275.00
Tracy	Beautiful Bride Tracy	1982	4103	$65.00
Tracy	Tracy Doll (Bridal)	1983	4103	$40.00
Truly	Talking Truly Scrumptious	1969	1107	$350.00
Truly	Truly Scrumptious (Straight Leg)	1969	1108	$400.00
Tutti	Cookin' Goodies	1967	3559	$300.00
Tutti	Me and My Dog	1966	3554	$250.00
Tutti	Melody In Pink #1	1966	3555	$200.00
Tutti	Melody In Pink #2 (different dress)	1966	3555	$200.00
Tutti	Night Night Sleep Tight	1966	3553	$150.00
Tutti	Night Night Sleep Tight (Europe)	1975	7455	$100.00
Tutti	Swing-A-Ling	1967	3560	$125.00
Tutti	Swing-A-Ling (Europe)	1975	7453	$125.00

Family & Friends Dolls

Listed by Doll

Doll	Item	Year	Number	Value
Tutti	Tutti Doll (blonde)	1966	3350	$75.00
Tutti	Tutti Doll (brunette)	1966	3350	$75.00
Tutti	Tutti Doll (different dress, brunette)	1967	3550	$40.00
Tutti	Tutti Doll (different dress, brunette)	1967	3580	$40.00
Tutti	Tutti (reissue, Europe)	1967	Foreign	$25.00
Tutti	Walking My Dolly	1966	3552	$150.00
Tutti	Walking My Dolly (Europe)	1975	7454	$100.00
Twiggy	Twiggy Doll	1967	1185	$350.00
Whitney	Happy Meal Whitney	1994	11476	$14.00
Whitney	Jewel Secrets Whitney	1987	3179	$45.00
Whitney	Perfume Pretty Whitney	1988	4557	$40.00
Whitney	Polly Pockets Whitney	1995	12983	$10.00
Whitney	Style Magic Whitney	1988	1280	$25.00
Whitney	Totally Hair Whitney	1992	7735	$45.00
Whitney	Wet 'n Wild Whitney	1990	4136	$80.00

FAMILY & FRIENDS DOLLS

Listed by Stock Number

NUMBER	ITEM	YEAR	VALUE	DOLL
0750	Ken Doll	1964	N/A	Ken
0950	Skipper Doll (Straight Leg)	1970	$175.00	Skipper
0950	Skipper Doll (Straight Leg, blonde)	1964	$125.00	Skipper
0950	Skipper Doll (Straight Leg, brunette)	1964	$125.00	Skipper
0950	Skipper Doll (Straight Leg, reissue)	1971	$72.00	Skipper
0950	Skipper Doll (Straight Leg, Titian)	1964	$125.00	Skipper
750	Ken Doll (1st issue, flocked, Straight Leg)	1961	$200.00	Ken
750	Ken Doll (blond)	1961	N/A	Ken
750	Ken Doll (brown)	1961	N/A	Ken
750	Ken Doll (brunet)	1961	N/A	Ken
750	Ken Doll (crew cut, blond)	1963	N/A	Ken
750	Ken Doll (crew cut, brunet)	1963	N/A	Ken
750	Ken Doll (painted brunett hair)	1962	N/A	Ken
750	Ken Doll (Straight Leg, flocked brunet)	1961	$180.00	Ken
750	Ken (Straight Leg, molded hair, ¼ shorter)	1963	$140.00	Ken
750	Ken (Straight Leg, molded hair painted blond)	1962	$95.00	Ken
860	Midge Doll (Bendable Leg)	1965	$500.00	Midge
860	Midge Doll (brunette)	1963	N/A	Midge
860	Midge Doll (no freckles)	1963	$400.00	Midge
860	Midge Doll (Straight Leg, brunette)	1963	$125.00	Midge
860	Midge Doll (Straight Leg with teeth, blonde)	1963	$125.00	Midge
860	Midge Doll (sunny blonde)	1963	N/A	Midge
860	Midge Doll (Titian)	1963	N/A	Midge
950	Ken Doll (Straight Leg, flocked)	1961	$200.00	Ken
1000	Allan Straight Legs (redhead)	1964	$98.00	Allan
1009	Wig Wardrobe Molded	1965	$225.00	Midge
1010	Allan (Bendable Leg)	1965	$300.00	Allan
1019	Scott Doll	1990	$45.00	Scott
1019	Super Teen Scott	1979	$50.00	Scott
1020	Ken Doll (Bendable Leg)	1965	300.00	Ken
1020	Ken Doll (Bendable Leg)	1969	$100.00	Ken
1020	Ken Doll (Bendable Leg, painted cheeks)	1965	N/A	Ken
1020	Tropical Ken	1986	$12.00	Ken
1021	Tropical Skipper	1986	$20.00	Skipper
1023	Tropical Ken (black)	1986	$15.00	Ken
1030	Skipper Doll (Bendable Leg)	1965	$175.00	Skipper
1030	Skipper Doll (Bendable Leg, blonde)	1965	N/A	Skipper
1030	Skipper Doll (Bendable Leg, reissue)	1967	$100.00	Skipper
1030	Skipper Doll (Bendable Leg, Titian)	1965	N/A	Skipper
1040	Skooter Doll (blonde)	1965	$150.00	Skooter

FAMILY & FRIENDS DOLLS

Listed by Stock Number

NUMBER	ITEM	YEAR	VALUE	DOLL
1040	Skooter Doll (brunette)	1965	$150.00	Skooter
1040	Skooter Doll (redhead)	1965	$150.00	Skooter
1068	Malibu Francie	1973	$45.00	Francie
1068	Malibu Francie	1978	$30.00	Francie
1068	Malibu Francie (new box)	1975	$40.00	Francie
1068	Malibu Francie (new rose box)	1976	$40.00	Francie
1068	Malibu Francie (The Sun Set)	1971	$30.00	Francie
1069	Malibu Skipper (new box)	1975	$70.00	Skipper
1069	Malibu Skipper (new rose box)	1976	$75.00	Skipper
1069	Malibu Skipper (The Sun Set)	1971	$15.00	Skipper
1069	Sun Gold Malibu Skipper	1984	$20.00	Skipper
1069	Sun Lovin' Malibu Skipper	1980	$30.00	Skipper
1069	Sunsational Malibu Skipper	1981	$15.00	Skipper
1069	Sunsational Malibu Skipper	1982	$30.00	Skipper
1074	Growin' Pretty Hair (extra hair pieces)	1971	$175.00	Francie
1080	Bendable Leg Midge	1965	$350.00	Midge
1080	Midge Doll (Bendable Leg, brunette)	1965	$550.00	Midge
1088	Malibu Ken (darker skin, new box)	1976	$50.00	Ken
1088	Malibu Ken (new box)	1975	$50.00	Ken
1088	Malibu Ken (new rose box)	1976	$50.00	Ken
1088	Malibu Ken (The Sun Set)	1971	$30.00	Ken
1088	Sun Gold Malibu Ken	1984	$20.00	Ken
1088	Sun Lovin' Malibu Ken	1979	$30.00	Ken
1088	Sunsational Malibu Ken	1981	$15.00	Ken
1088	Sunsational Malibu Ken	1982	$30.00	Ken
1090	Ricky (redhead)	1965	$150.00	Ricky
1100	Francie Doll 1st issue (black, red oxidized)	1967	$900.00	Francie
1100	Francie Doll 2nd issue (black, dark brown)	1967	$800.00	Francie
1100	Twist 'n Turn Francie (black)	1967	$985.00	Francie
1105	Twist 'n Turn Skipper	1970	$100.00	Skipper
1105	Twist 'n Turn Skipper (new 2 curl hairstyle)	1969	$100.00	Skipper
1107	Talking Truly Scrumptious	1969	$350.00	Truly
1108	Truly Scrumptious (Straight Leg)	1969	$400.00	Truly
1111	Talking Ken	1973	$20.00	Ken
1111	Talking Ken (Baggie, non-talking)	1969	$100.00	Ken
1113	Talking P.J.	1969	$155.00	P.J.
1113	Talking P.J. (Baggie, non-talking)	1973	$20.00	P.J.
1114	Talking Brad	1970	$125.00	Brad
1114	Talking Brad (darker skin)	1971	$125.00	Brad
1115	Totally Hair Ken	1992	$30.00	Ken

FAMILY & FRIENDS DOLLS

Listed by Stock Number

NUMBER	ITEM	YEAR	VALUE	DOLL
1117	Living Skipper (new clothes)	1971	$80.00	Skipper
1117	Malibu Skipper (Baggie)	1973	$30.00	Skipper
1117	New Living Skipper	1970	$150.00	Skipper
1117	Pose 'n Play Skipper (Baggie)	1973	$30.00	Skipper
1118	Twist 'n Turn P.J.	1970	$100.00	P.J.
1119	Twist 'n Turn Christie	1970	$150.00	Christie
1120	Skooter Doll (pink, Bendable Leg)	1966	$175.00	Skooter
1120	Skooter Doll (tan, Bendable Leg)	1966	$150.00	Skooter
1122	Hair Happenin's Francie	1970	$250.00	Francie
1124	Ken Doll (Bendable Leg)	1970	$100.00	Ken
1125	Talking Stacey	1968	$290.00	Stacey
1125	Talking Stacey (blue/silver suite)	1970	$365.00	Stacey
1125	Talking Stacey (new window box)	1969	$350.00	Stacey
1126	Talking Christie	1968	$150.00	Christie
1126	Talking Christie (darker skin)	1971	$150.00	Christie
1126	Talking Christie (new window box)	1969	$150.00	Christie
1127	Twist 'n Turn Julia	1969	$150.00	Julia
1128	Talking Julia	1969	$150.00	Julia
1128	Talking Julia (darker skin)	1971	$150.00	Julia
1129	Growin' Pretty Hair Francie	1970	$200.00	Francie
1130	Francie Doll 2nd issue (blonde)	1966	N/A	Francie
1130	Francie Doll 2nd issue (brunette)	1966	N/A	Francie
1130	Francie Doll (Bendable Leg)	1966	$250.00	Francie
1132	Walking Jamie	1970	$250.00	Jamie
1133	Pretty Pairs Lori 'n Rori	1970	$200.00	Lori
1134	Pretty Pairs Nan 'n Fran	1970	$200.00	Nan
1135	Pretty Pairs Angie 'n Tangie	1970	$255.00	Angie
1140	Francie Doll (Straight Legs blonde)	1966	$300.00	Francie
1140	Francie Doll (Straight Legs brunette)	1966	$175.00	Francie
1142	Brad Doll (Bendable Leg)	1970	$150.00	Brad
1142	Brad Doll (Bendable Leg, darker skin)	1971	$135.00	Brad
1143	Living Fluff	1971	$175.00	Fluff
1147	Trade-In Special Living Skipper	1970	$125.00	Skipper
1153	Live Action on Stage P.J.	1971	$215.00	P.J.
1153	Living Skipper (blonde)	1970	$85.00	Skipper
1156	Live Action P.J.	1971	$100.00	P.J.
1156	Live Action P.J. (Baggie)	1973	$36.00	P.J.
1159	Ken (Baggie, Talking Body-Live Action Head)	1974	$45.00	Ken
1159	Live Action Ken	1971	$100.00	Ken
1159	Live Action Ken (Baggie)	1973	$27.00	Ken

FAMILY & FRIENDS DOLLS

Listed by Stock Number

NUMBER	ITEM	YEAR	VALUE	DOLL
1165	Twist 'n Turn Stacey (aqua/rose suit)	1970	$332.00	Stacey
1165	Twist 'n Turn Stacey (blonde)	1969	$298.00	Stacey
1165	Twist 'n Turn Stacey (brunette, new box)	1969	$295.00	Stacey
1165	Twist 'n Turn Stacey (Titian)	1968	$300.00	Stacey
1170	Twist 'n Turn Francie	1969	$325.00	Francie
1170	Twist 'n Turn Francie (blonde)	1967	$75.00	Francie
1170	Twist 'n Turn Francie (brunette)	1967	$75.00	Francie
1170	Twist 'n Turn Francie (no bangs, blonde)	1971	$500.00	Francie
1170	Twist 'n Turn Francie (no bangs, brunette)	1971	$500.00	Francie
1172	Live Action on Stage Ken	1971	$150.00	Ken
1175	Live Action Christie	1971	$150.00	Christie
1179	Pose 'n Play Swing-A-Round	1972	$300.00	Skipper
1180	Casey Doll (blonde)	1967	$300.00	Casey
1180	Casey Doll (brunette)	1967	$300.00	Casey
1180	Twist 'n Turn Casey (blonde)	1969	$300.00	Casey
1180	Twist 'n Turn Casey (brunette)	1969	$300.00	Casey
1183	Walk Lively Steffie	1972	$150.00	Steffie
1184	Walk Lively Ken	1972	$80.00	Ken
1185	Twiggy Doll	1967	$350.00	Twiggy
1186	Talking Busy Steffie with Holdin' Hands	1972	$250.00	Steffie
1187	Malibu P.J. (Baggie)	1973	$20.00	P.J.
1187	Malibu P.J. (new box)	1975	$70.00	P.J.
1187	Malibu P.J. (The Sun Set)	1971	$30.00	P.J.
1187	Sun Gold Malibu P.J.	1984	$20.00	P.J.
1187	Sun Lovin' Malibu P.J.	1980	$30.00	P.J.
1187	Sunsational Malibu P.J.	1981	$25.00	P.J.
1187	Sunsational Malibu P.J.	1982	$30.00	P.J.
1194	Rise 'n Shine	1971	N/A	Francie
1196	Rocker Dana	1986	$30.00	Dana
1196	Talking Busy Ken	1972	$200.00	Ken
1199	Pose 'n Play Tiff	1972	$300.00	Tiff
1247	Walking Jamie Strollin' In Style	1972	$450.00	Jamie
1248	Malibu Ken Surf's Up	1971	$30.00	Ken
1280	Style Magic Whitney	1988	$25.00	Whitney
1290	Style Magic Christie	1989	$25.00	Christie
1294	Sport & Shave Ken	1980	$30.00	Ken
1295	Beauty Secrets Christie	1980	$45.00	Christie
1295	Pretty Reflections Christie	1979	$85.00	Christie
1351	Animal Lovin' Ken	1989	$35.00	Ken
1352	Animal Lovin' Nikki	1989	$35.00	Nikki

Family & Friends Dolls

Listed by Stock Number

Number	Item	Year	Value	Doll
1389	My First Ken	1989	$15.00	Ken
1392	Sun Sensation Ken	1992	$15.00	Ken
1393	Sun Sensation Christie	1992	$15.00	Christie
1396	Sun Sensation Steven	1992	$15.00	Steven
1446	Sun Sensation Skipper	1992	$15.00	Skipper
1447	Sun Sensation Kira	1992	$15.00	Kira
1503	My First Ken	1993	Rtl	Ken
1535	Superstar Ken	1989	$35.00	Ken
1550	Superstar Ken (black)	1989	$35.00	Ken
1599	Baby Sitter Skipper (black)	1991	$14.00	Skipper
1719	Jewel Secrets Ken	1987	$25.00	Ken
1881	Roller Skating Ken	1981	$50.00	Ken
1915	Style Magic Skipper	1989	$30.00	Skipper
1950	Homecoming Queen Skipper	1989	$45.00	Skipper
1951	Teentime Skipper	1989	N/A	Skipper
1952	Teentime Courtney	1989	$25.00	Courtney
2056	Tropical Miko	1986	$20.00	Miko
2215	Rollerblade Ken	1992	$30.00	Ken
2216	Rollerblade Teresa	1992	$30.00	Teresa
2217	Rollerblade Christie	1992	$30.00	Christie
2218	Rollerblade Kira	1992	$30.00	Kira
2250	Dream Glow Ken	1986	$25.00	Ken
2290	Earring Magic Ken	1993	$25.00	Ken
2309	Hollywood Hair Skipper	1993	Rtl	Skipper
2316	Hollywood Hair Teresa	1993	Rtl	Teresa
2323	Fashion Photo P.J.	1978	$60.00	P.J.
2388	Music Lovin' Ken	1985	$45.00	Ken
2390	Homecoming Queen Skipper (black)	1989	$45.00	Skipper
2421	Dream Glow Ken (black)	1986	$25.00	Ken
2427	Rocker Diva	1986	$30.00	Diva
2428	Rocker Derek	1986	$30.00	Derek
2701	Pet Pals Courtney	1992	$20.00	Courtney
2711	Pet Pals Kevin	1992	$20.00	Kevin
2752	The Beat Christie	1990	$25.00	Christie
2754	The Beat Midge	1990	$25.00	Midge
2756	Super Teen Skipper	1980	$30.00	Skipper
2820	Wedding Day Kelly & Todd	1991	$35.00	Kelly
2854	Music Lovin' Skipper	1985	$65.00	Skipper
2955	Kissing Christie	1980	$50.00	Christie
2960	Hawaiian Ken	1981	$50.00	Ken

FAMILY & FRIENDS DOLLS

Listed by Stock Number

Number	Item	Year	Value	Doll
3131	Rocker Hot Rockin' Ken	1986	$35.00	Ken
3131	Rocker Ken	1986	$30.00	Ken
3131	Rocker Ken (revised)	1987	$30.00	Ken
3133	Jewel Secrets Skipper	1987	$25.00	Skipper
3137	Rocker Derek (revised)	1987	$30.00	Derek
3149	Sparkle Eyes Ken	1992	$25.00	Ken
3149	Sparkle Surprise Ken	1992	N/A	Ken
3158	Rocker Dana (revised)	1987	$30.00	Dana
3158	Rocker Dancin' Action Dana	1986	$35.00	Dana
3159	Rocker Dancin' Action Diva	1986	$35.00	Diva
3159	Rocker Diva (revised)	1987	$30.00	Diva
3160	Rocker Dancin' Action Dee Dee	1986	$35.00	Dee Dee
3160	Rocker Dee Dee	1986	$30.00	Dee Dee
3160	Rocker Dee Dee (revised)	1987	$30.00	Dee Dee
3173	Rocker Hot Rockin' Derek	1986	$35.00	Derek
3179	Jewel Secrets Whitney	1987	$45.00	Whitney
3200	Walk Lively Miss America	1972	$75.00	Miss America
3215	Cool Times Ken	1989	$20.00	Ken
3216	Cool Times Midge	1989	$20.00	Midge
3217	Cool Times Christie	1989	$20.00	Christie
3218	Cool Times Teresa	1989	$20.00	Teresa
3232	Jewel Secrets Ken (black)	1987	$25.00	Ken
3238	Beach Blast Ken	1989	$15.00	Ken
3242	Beach Blast Skipper	1989	$15.00	Skipper
3244	Beach Blast Miko	1989	$15.00	Miko
3249	Beach Blast Teresa	1989	$15.00	Teresa
3249	Golden Dream Christie	1981	$50.00	Christie
3251	Beach Blast Steven	1989	$15.00	Steven
3253	Beach Blast Christie	1989	$25.00	Christie
3265	Rappin' Rockin' Christie	1992	$25.00	Christie
3270	Rappin' Rockin' Teresa	1992	$25.00	Teresa
3312	Busy Steffie	1972	$200.00	Steffie
3313	Busy Francie with Holdin' Hands	1972	$300.00	Francie
3314	Busy Ken	1972	$150.00	Ken
3350	Tutti Doll (blonde)	1966	$75.00	Tutti
3350	Tutti Doll (brunette)	1966	$75.00	Tutti
3357	Buffy and Mrs. Beasley	1968	$175.00	Buffy
3511	Dance Club Ken	1989	$35.00	Ken
3512	Dance Club Kayla	1989	$35.00	Kayla
3513	Dance Club Devon	1989	$35.00	Devon

FAMILY & FRIENDS DOLLS

Listed by Stock Number

NUMBER	ITEM	YEAR	VALUE	DOLL
3550	Tutti Doll (different dress, brunette)	1967	$40.00	Tutti
3552	Walking My Dolly	1966	$150.00	Tutti
3553	All Star Ken	1982	$25.00	Ken
3553	Night Night Sleep Tight	1966	$150.00	Tutti
3554	Me and My Dog	1966	$250.00	Tutti
3554	Pink & Pretty Christie	1981	$45.00	Christie
3555	Melody In Pink #1	1966	$200.00	Tutti
3555	Melody In Pink #2 (different dress)	1966	$200.00	Tutti
3555	Pink and Pretty Christie	1982	$40.00	Christie
3556	Tutti and Todd Sundae Treat Play Set	1966	$275.00	Todd
3559	Cookin' Goodies	1967	$300.00	Tutti
3560	Swing-A-Ling	1967	$125.00	Tutti
3570	Chris Doll (blond)	1967	$75.00	Chris
3570	Chris Doll (brunet)	1967	$150.00	Chris
3580	Todd Doll	1966	$160.00	Todd
3580	Tutti Doll (different dress, brunette)	1967	$40.00	Tutti
3590	Todd Doll (Titian)	1967	$65.00	Todd
3600	Horse Lovin' Ken	1983	$45.00	Ken
3600	Western Ken	1982	$30.00	Ken
3631	Cheerleader Jazzie	1988	$25.00	Jazzie
3632	Swim Suit Jazzie	1988	$25.00	Jazzie
3633	Workout Jazzie	1988	N/A	Jazzie
3634	Teen Dance Jazzie	1988	$25.00	Jazzie
3635	High School Jazzie	1988	$25.00	Jazzie
3636	High School Stacey	1988	$25.00	Stacey
3637	High School Dude	1988	$40.00	Dude
3698	High School Chelsie	1988	$40.00	Chelsie
3841	My First Ken	1992	$15.00	Ken
3849	Sun Gold Malibu Ken (black)	1985	$20.00	Ken
3849	Sunsational Malibu Ken (black)	1982	$30.00	Ken
3849	Sunsational Malibu Ken with Hair	1981	$40.00	Ken
3876	My First Ken (black)	1993	Rtl	Ken
3931	Baton Twirling Skipper	1993	$10.00	Skipper
3933	Cheerleading Courtney	1993	$10.00	Courtney
4049	Pet Pals Skipper	1992	$20.00	Skipper
4049	Pet Pals Skipper (black)	1992	$20.00	Skipper
4060	Island Fun Ken	1988	$35.00	Ken
4064	Island Fun Skipper	1988	$25.00	Skipper
4065	Island Fun Miko	1988	$25.00	Miko
4077	Dream Date Ken	1983	$30.00	Ken

Family & Friends Dolls

Listed by Stock Number

Number	Item	Year	Value	Doll
4088	Sun Lovin' Malibu Jazzie	1990	$20.00	Jazzie
4093	Island Fun Christie	1988	$25.00	Christie
4093	Island Fun Steven	1988	$25.00	Steven
4103	Beautiful Bride Tracy	1982	$65.00	Tracy
4103	Tracy Doll (Bridal)	1983	$40.00	Tracy
4104	Wet 'n Wild Ken	1990	$20.00	Ken
4115	Party 'n Play Stacie (black)	1993	Rtl	Stacie
4117	Island Fun Teresa	1988	$25.00	Teresa
4118	Doctor Ken	1987	$25.00	Ken
4118	Dr. Ken	1987	$25.00	Ken
4120	Wet 'n Wild Kira	1990	$20.00	Kira
4121	Wet 'n Wild Christie	1990	$20.00	Christie
4136	Wet 'n Wild Teresa	1990	$20.00	Teresa
4136	Wet 'n Wild Whitney	1990	$80.00	Whitney
4137	Wet 'n Wild Steven	1990	$20.00	Steven
4138	Wet 'n Wild Skipper	1990	$20.00	Skipper
4221	Quick Curl Kelley	1973	$80.00	Kelley
4222	Quick Curl Francie	1973	$75.00	Francie
4223	Quick Curl Skipper	1973	$30.00	Skipper
4224	Mod Hair Ken	1973	$65.00	Ken
4234	Mod Hair Ken	1974	$45.00	Ken
4240	Littlest Sister Stacie	1992	$20.00	Stacie
4253	Handsome Groom Todd	1983	$40.00	Todd
4431	Barbie & Friends P.J.	1983	$40.00	P.J.
4441	California Dream Ken	1988	$20.00	Ken
4442	California Dream Midge	1988	$20.00	Midge
4443	California Dream Christie	1988	$25.00	Christie
4554	Perfume Giving Ken	1988	N/A	Ken
4554	Perfume Pretty Ken	1987	$30.00	Ken
4555	Perfume Giving Ken (black)	1988	N/A	Ken
4555	Perfume Pretty Ken (black)	1987	$30.00	Ken
4557	Perfume Pretty Whitney	1988	$40.00	Whitney
4713	Basketball Kevin	1993	$10.00	Kevin
4817	Dream Date Skipper	1990	$30.00	Skipper
4829	Hollywood Hair Ken	1993	$23.00	Ken
4849	Dream Date Skipper (black)	1990	$30.00	Skipper
4855	Teen Sweetheart Skipper	1988	N/A	Skipper
4867	Pepsi Spirit Skipper	1989	$50.00	Skipper
4876	Benetton Shopping Ken	1992	$50.00	Ken
4880	Benetton Shopping Teresa	1992	$50.00	Teresa

FAMILY & FRIENDS DOLLS

Listed by Stock Number

NUMBER	ITEM	YEAR	VALUE	DOLL
4887	Benetton Shopping Christie	1992	$50.00	Christie
4898	Benetton Shopping Marina	1992	$50.00	Marina
4898	Crystal Ken	1984	$25.00	Ken
4903	Rappin' Rockin' Ken	1992	$25.00	Ken
4904	Glitter Beach Ken	1993	$5.00	Ken
4907	Glitter Beach Christie	1993	$25.00	Christie
4918	Glitter Beach Steven	1993	$5.00	Steven
4920	Glitter Beach Skipper	1993	$5.00	Skipper
4921	Glitter Beach Teresa	1993	$5.00	Teresa
4924	Glitter Beach Kira	1993	$5.00	Kira
4935	Glitter Beach Jazzie	1993	$5.00	Jazzie
4967	The Sensations Bopsy	1988	$25.00	Bopsy
4971	Sun Gold Malibu Ken (Hispanic)	1984	$20.00	Ken
4971	Sunsational Malibu Ken (Hispanic)	1983	$40.00	Ken
4976	The Sensations Belinda	1988	$25.00	Belinda
4977	The Sensations Becky	1988	$25.00	Becky
4989	Cool Tops Skipper	1990	$20.00	Skipper
5029	Horse Lovin' Skipper	1983	$45.00	Skipper
5029	Western Skipper	1982	$30.00	Skipper
5316	Fashion Jeans Ken	1982	$50.00	Ken
5411	Party 'n Play Stacie	1993	Rtl	Stacie
5441	Cool Tops Skipper (black)	1990	$10.00	Skipper
5473	Sun Sensation Jazzie	1992	$15.00	Jazzie
5503	California Dream Teresa	1988	$20.00	Teresa
5619	Army Ken (black)	1993	$20.00	Ken
5839	Super Sport Ken	1982	$25.00	Ken
5869	Dream Date P.J.	1983	$30.00	P.J.
5893	Cheerleader Teen Skipper	1988	$25.00	Skipper
5899	Party Teen Doll	1988	N/A	Skipper
5899	Workout Teen Doll	1988	N/A	Skipper
5941	Hawaiian Fun Ken	1991	$10.00	Ken
5942	Hawaiian Fun Skipper	1991	$10.00	Skipper
5943	Hawaiian Fun Kira	1991	$10.00	Kira
5944	Hawaiian Fun Christie	1991	$10.00	Christie
5945	Hawaiian Fun Steven	1991	$10.00	Steven
7079	Cool Tops Courtney	1990	$20.00	Courtney
7081	Dance Magic Ken	1990	$25.00	Ken
7082	Dance Magic Ken (black)	1990	$25.00	Ken
7154	Costume Ball Ken	1991	$25.00	Ken
7160	Costume Ball Ken (black)	1991	$25.00	Ken

FAMILY & FRIENDS DOLLS

Listed by Stock Number

NUMBER	ITEM	YEAR	VALUE	DOLL
7193	Funtime Skipper	1975	N/A	Skipper
7193	Funtime Skipper (Germany)	1975	N/A	Skipper
7194	Funtime Ken	1975	$25.00	Ken
7194	Funtime Ken (Germany)	1975	N/A	Ken
7259	Growing Up Skipper (long pale blonde)	1975	$60.00	Skipper
7259	Growing Up Skipper (short golden blonde)	1975	$65.00	Skipper
7261	Gold Medal Skier Ken	1975	$75.00	Ken
7263	Gold Medal Gymnast P.J.	1975	$85.00	P.J.
7263	Gymnast P.J.	1974	$75.00	P.J.
7280	Free Moving Ken	1975	$50.00	Ken
7281	Free Moving P.J.	1975	$50.00	P.J.
7281	Malibu P.J. (new rose box)	1976	$75.00	P.J.
7282	Free Moving Curtis	1975	$50.00	Curtis
7283	Free Moving Cara	1975	$30.00	Cara
7291	Quick Curl Cara	1975	$35.00	Cara
7318	Great Shape Ken	1984	$25.00	Ken
7375	Ice Capades Ken	1990	$25.00	Ken
7377	Carla	1976	$150.00	Carla
7377	Carla (Europe)	1976	$45.00	Carla
7377	Carla (reissue Europe)	1976	$50.00	Carla
7381	Funtime Skooter (Europe)	1976	N/A	Skooter
7414	Great Shape Skipper	1984	$30.00	Skipper
7453	Swing-A-Ling (Europe)	1975	$125.00	Tutti
7454	Walking My Dolly (Europe)	1975	$100.00	Tutti
7455	Night Night Sleep Tight (Europe)	1975	$100.00	Tutti
7455	Sweet Roses P.J.	1984	$45.00	P.J.
7495	Hawaiian Ken	1983	$40.00	Ken
7512	Ski Fun Ken	1992	$20.00	Ken
7513	Ski Fun Midge	1992	$50.00	Midge
7574	Marine Ken	1991	$25.00	Ken
7594	Marine Ken (black)	1992	$25.00	Ken
7699	Francie Doll (Baggie)	1975	$40.00	Francie
7735	Totally Hair Whitney	1992	$45.00	Whitney
7745	Malibu Christie	1975	$35.00	Christie
7745	Malibu Christie (new box)	1975	$35.00	Christie
7745	Malibu Christie (new rose box)	1976	$75.00	Christie
7745	Malibue Christie	1978	$30.00	Christie
7745	Sun Lovin' Malibu Christie	1980	$30.00	Christie
7745	Sunsational Malibu Christie	1981	$20.00	Christie
7745	Sunsational Malibu Christie	1982	$30.00	Christie

FAMILY & FRIENDS DOLLS

Listed by Year

YEAR	ITEM	NUMBER	VALUE	DOLL
1966	Francie Doll (Straight Legs blonde)	1140	$300.00	Francie
1966	Francie Doll (Straight Legs brunette)	1140	$175.00	Francie
1966	Me and My Dog	3554	$250.00	Tutti
1966	Melody In Pink #1	3555	$200.00	Tutti
1966	Melody In Pink #2 (different dress)	3555	$200.00	Tutti
1966	Night Night Sleep Tight	3553	$150.00	Tutti
1966	Skooter Doll (pink, Bendable Leg)	1120	$175.00	Skooter
1966	Skooter Doll (tan, Bendable Leg)	1120	$150.00	Skooter
1966	Todd Doll	3580	$160.00	Todd
1966	Tutti And Todd Sundae Treat Play Set	3556	$275.00	Todd
1966	Tutti Doll (blonde)	3350	$75.00	Tutti
1966	Tutti Doll (brunette)	3350	$75.00	Tutti
1966	Walking My Dolly	3552	$150.00	Tutti
1967	Casey Doll (blonde)	1180	$300.00	Casey
1967	Casey Doll (brunette)	1180	$300.00	Casey
1967	Chris Doll (blond)	3570	$75.00	Chris
1967	Chris Doll (brunet)	3570	$150.00	Chris
1967	Cookin' Goodies	3559	$300.00	Tutti
1967	Francie Doll 1st issue (black, red oxidized)	1100	$900.00	Francie
1967	Francie Doll 2nd issue (black, dark brown)	1100	$800.00	Francie
1967	Skipper Doll (Bendable Leg, reissue)	1030	$100.00	Skipper
1967	Swing-A-Ling	3560	$125.00	Tutti
1967	Todd Doll (Titian)	3590	$65.00	Todd
1967	Todd (reissue, Europe)	Foreign	$25.00	Todd
1967	Tutti Doll (different dress, brunette)	3550	$40.00	Tutti
1967	Tutti Doll (different dress, brunette)	3580	$40.00	Tutti
1967	Tutti (reissue, Europe)	Foreign	$25.00	Tutti
1967	Twiggy Doll	1185	$350.00	Twiggy
1967	Twist 'n Turn Francie (black)	1100	$985.00	Francie
1967	Twist 'n Turn Francie (blonde)	1170	$75.00	Francie
1967	Twist 'n Turn Francie (brunette)	1170	$75.00	Francie
1968	Buffy and Mrs. Beasley	3357	$175.00	Buffy
1968	Talking Christie	1126	$150.00	Christie
1968	Talking Stacey	1125	$290.00	Stacey
1968	Twist 'n Turn Stacey (Titian)	1165	$300.00	Stacey
1969	Ken Doll (Bendable Leg)	1020	$100.00	Ken
1969	New 'n Groovy Talking P.J.	N/A	$150.00	P.J.
1969	Talking Christie (new window box)	1126	$150.00	Christie
1969	Talking Julia	1128	$150.00	Julia
1969	Talking Ken	1111	$100.00	Ken

FAMILY & FRIENDS DOLLS

Listed by Year

YEAR	ITEM	NUMBER	VALUE	DOLL
1969	Talking P.J.	1113	$155.00	P.J.
1969	Talking Stacey (new window box)	1125	$350.00	Stacey
1969	Talking Truly Scrumptious	1107	$350.00	Truly
1969	Truly Scrumptious (Straight Leg)	1108	$400.00	Truly
1969	Twist 'n Turn Casey (blonde)	1180	$300.00	Casey
1969	Twist 'n Turn Casey (brunette)	1180	$300.00	Casey
1969	Twist 'n Turn Francie	1170	$325.00	Francie
1969	Twist 'n Turn Julia	1127	$150.00	Julia
1969	Twist 'n Turn Skipper (new 2 curl hairstyle)	1105	$100.00	Skipper
1969	Twist 'n Turn Stacey (blonde)	1165	$298.00	Stacey
1969	Twist 'n Turn Stacey (brunette, new box)	1165	$295.00	Stacey
1970	Bendable Leg Ken Gift Set	1436	N/A	Ken
1970	Brad Doll (Bendable Leg)	1142	$150.00	Brad
1970	Growin' Pretty Hair Francie	1129	$200.00	Francie
1970	Hair Happenin's Francie	1122	$250.00	Francie
1970	Ken Doll (Bendable Leg)	1124	$100.00	Ken
1970	Living Skipper (blonde)	1153	$85.00	Skipper
1970	New Living Skipper	1117	$150.00	Skipper
1970	Pretty Pairs Angie 'n Tangie	1135	$255.00	Angie
1970	Pretty Pairs Lori 'n Rori	1133	$200.00	Lori
1970	Pretty Pairs Nan 'n Fran	1134	$200.00	Nan
1970	Skipper Doll (Straight Leg)	0950	$175.00	Skipper
1970	Spanish Talking Ken	8372	$200.00	Ken
1970	Talking Brad	1114	$125.00	Brad
1970	Talking Stacey (blue/silver suite)	1125	$365.00	Stacey
1970	Trade-In Special Living Skipper	1147	$125.00	Skipper
1970	Twist 'n Turn Christie	1119	$150.00	Christie
1970	Twist 'n Turn P.J.	1118	$100.00	P.J.
1970	Twist 'n Turn Skipper	1105	$100.00	Skipper
1970	Twist 'n Turn Stacey (aqua/rose suit)	1165	$332.00	Stacey
1970	Walking Jamie	1132	$250.00	Jamie
1971	Brad Doll (Bendable Leg, darker skin)	1142	$135.00	Brad
1971	Francie (Germany)	Foreign	N/A	Francie
1971	Growin' Pretty Hair (extra hair pieces)	1074	$175.00	Francie
1971	Live Action Christie	1175	$150.00	Christie
1971	Live Action Ken	1159	$100.00	Ken
1971	Live Action on Stage Ken	1172	$150.00	Ken
1971	Live Action on Stage P.J.	1153	$215.00	P.J.
1971	Live Action P.J.	1156	$100.00	P.J.
1971	Living Fluff	1143	$175.00	Fluff

FAMILY & FRIENDS DOLLS

Listed by Year

YEAR	ITEM	NUMBER	VALUE	DOLL
1971	Living Skipper (new clothes)	1117	$80.00	Skipper
1971	Malibu Francie (The Sun Set)	1068	$30.00	Francie
1971	Malibu Ken Surf's Up	1248	$30.00	Ken
1971	Malibu Ken (The Sun Set)	1088	$30.00	Ken
1971	Malibu P.J. (The Sun Set)	1187	$30.00	P.J.
1971	Malibu Skipper (The Sun Set)	1069	$15.00	Skipper
1971	Rise 'n Shine	1194	N/A	Francie
1971	Skipper Doll (Straight Leg, reissue)	0950	$72.00	Skipper
1971	Talking Brad (darker skin)	1114	$125.00	Brad
1971	Talking Christie (darker skin)	1126	$150.00	Christie
1971	Talking Julia (darker skin)	1128	$150.00	Julia
1971	Twist 'n Turn Francie (no bangs, blonde)	1170	$500.00	Francie
1971	Twist 'n Turn Francie (no bangs, brunette)	1170	$500.00	Francie
1972	Busy Francie with Holdin' Hands	3313	$300.00	Francie
1972	Busy Ken	3314	$150.00	Ken
1972	Busy Steffie	3312	$200.00	Steffie
1972	Pose 'n Play Swing-A-Round	1179	$300.00	Skipper
1972	Pose 'n Play Tiff	1199	$300.00	Tiff
1972	Talking Busy Ken	1196	$200.00	Ken
1972	Talking Busy Steffie with Holdin' Hands	1186	$250.00	Steffie
1972	Walk Lively Ken	1184	$80.00	Ken
1972	Walk Lively Miss America	3200	$75.00	Miss America
1972	Walk Lively Steffie	1183	$150.00	Steffie
1972	Walking Jamie Strollin' In Style	1247	$450.00	Jamie
1973	Live Action Ken (Baggie)	1159	$27.00	Ken
1973	Live Action P.J. (Baggie)	1156	$36.00	P.J.
1973	Malibu Francie	1068	$45.00	Francie
1973	Malibu P.J. (Baggie)	1187	$20.00	P.J.
1973	Malibu Skipper (Baggie)	1117	$30.00	Skipper
1973	Mod Hair Ken	4224	$65.00	Ken
1973	Pose 'n Play Skipper (Baggie)	1117	$30.00	Skipper
1973	Quick Curl Cara (Canada)	Foreign	$50.00	Cara
1973	Quick Curl Francie	4222	$75.00	Francie
1973	Quick Curl Kelley	4221	$80.00	Kelley
1973	Quick Curl Miss America (blonde)	8697	$55.00	Miss America
1973	Quick Curl Miss America (brunette)	8697	$210.00	Miss America
1973	Quick Curl Miss America (Canada)	8697	$90.00	Miss America
1973	Quick Curl Skipper	4223	$30.00	Skipper
1973	Talking Ken (Baggie, non-talking)	1111	$20.00	Ken
1973	Talking P.J. (Baggie, non-talking)	1113	$20.00	P.J.

Family & Friends Dolls

Listed by Year

Year	Item	Number	Value	Doll
1974	Chris (reissue Europe)	81300	$75.00	Chris
1974	Gymnast P.J.	7263	$75.00	P.J.
1974	Ken (Baggie, Talking Body-Live Action Head)	1159	$45.00	Ken
1974	Mod Hair Ken	4234	$45.00	Ken
1974	Quick Curl Miss America (blonde)	8697	N/A	Miss America
1974	Sun Valley Ken	7809	$125.00	Ken
1974	Yellowstone Kelley	7808	$200.00	Kelley
1975	Casey Doll (Baggie)	9000	$40.00	Casey
1975	Deluxe Quick Curl Skipper	9428	$65.00	Skipper
1975	Francie Doll (Baggie)	7699	$40.00	Francie
1975	Free Moving Cara	7283	$30.00	Cara
1975	Free Moving Curtis	7282	$50.00	Curtis
1975	Free Moving Ken	7280	$50.00	Ken
1975	Free Moving P.J.	7281	$50.00	P.J.
1975	Funtime Ken	7194	$25.00	Ken
1975	Funtime Ken (Germany)	7194	N/A	Ken
1975	Funtime Skipper	7193	N/A	Skipper
1975	Funtime Skipper (Germany)	7193	N/A	Skipper
1975	Gold Medal Gymnast P.J.	7263	$85.00	P.J.
1975	Gold Medal Skier Ken	7261	$75.00	Ken
1975	Growing Up Skipper (long pale blonde)	7259	$60.00	Skipper
1975	Growing Up Skipper (short golden blonde)	7259	$65.00	Skipper
1975	Malibu Christie	7745	$35.00	Christie
1975	Malibu Christie (new box)	7745	$35.00	Christie
1975	Malibu Francie (new box)	1068	$40.00	Francie
1975	Malibu Ken (new box)	1088	$50.00	Ken
1975	Malibu P.J. (new box)	1187	$70.00	P.J.
1975	Malibu Skipper (new box)	1069	$70.00	Skipper
1975	Night Night Sleep Tight (Europe)	7455	$100.00	Tutti
1975	Quick Curl Cara	7291	$35.00	Cara
1975	Swing-A-Ling (Europe)	7453	$125.00	Tutti
1975	Walking My Dolly (Europe)	7454	$100.00	Tutti
1976	Ballerina Cara	9528	$60.00	Cara
1976	Carla	7377	$150.00	Carla
1976	Carla (Europe)	7377	$45.00	Carla
1976	Carla (reissue Europe)	7377	$50.00	Carla
1976	Deluxe Quick Curl Cara	9220	$60.00	Cara
1976	Deluxe Quick Curl P.J.	9218	$60.00	P.J.
1976	Deluxe Quick Curl Skipper (Europe)	9428	$60.00	Skipper
1976	Funtime Skooter (Europe)	7381	N/A	Skooter

FAMILY & FRIENDS DOLLS

Listed by Year

YEAR	ITEM	NUMBER	VALUE	DOLL
1976	Growing Up Ginger	9222	$60.00	Ginger
1976	Malibu Christie (new rose box)	7745	$75.00	Christie
1976	Malibu Francie (new rose box)	1068	$40.00	Francie
1976	Malibu Ken (darker skin, new box)	1088	$50.00	Ken
1976	Malibu Ken (new rose box)	1088	$50.00	Ken
1976	Malibu P.J. (new rose box)	7281	$75.00	P.J.
1976	Malibu Skipper (new rose box)	1069	$75.00	Skipper
1976	Now Look Ken (longer hair)	9342	$45.00	Ken
1976	Now Look Ken (shorter hair)	9342	$65.00	Ken
1976	Quick Curl Miss America	8697	$75.00	Miss America
1976	Super Star Christie	N/A	$80.00	Christie
1976	Super Star Ken with Ring (1st issue)	N/A	$75.00	Ken
1977	Super Star Ken with Free Gift	N/A	$72.00	Ken
1978	Fashion Photo Christie	N/A	$60.00	Christie
1978	Fashion Photo P.J.	2323	$60.00	P.J.
1978	Malibu Francie	1068	$30.00	Francie
1978	Malibue Christie	7745	$30.00	Christie
1979	Pretty Reflections Christie	1295	$85.00	Christie
1979	Sports Star Ken (Canada)	Foreign	$40.00	Ken
1979	Sun Lovin' Malibu Ken	1088	$30.00	Ken
1979	Super Teen Scott	1019	$50.00	Scott
1980	Beauty Secrets Christie	1295	$45.00	Christie
1980	Golden Night Ken (Canada)	Foreign	$35.00	Ken
1980	Kissing Christie	2955	$50.00	Christie
1980	Sport & Shave Ken	1294	$30.00	Ken
1980	Sun Lovin' Malibu Christie	7745	$30.00	Christie
1980	Sun Lovin' Malibu P.J.	1187	$30.00	P.J.
1980	Sun Lovin' Malibu Skipper	1069	$30.00	Skipper
1980	Super Teen Skipper	2756	$30.00	Skipper
1981	Golden Dream Christie	3249	$50.00	Christie
1981	Hawaiian Ken	2960	$50.00	Ken
1981	Jogging Ken (Canada)	Foreign	$30.00	Ken
1981	Pink & Pretty Christie	3554	$45.00	Christie
1981	Roller Skating Ken	1881	$50.00	Ken
1981	Sunsational Malibu Christie	7745	$20.00	Christie
1981	Sunsational Malibu Ken	1088	$15.00	Ken
1981	Sunsational Malibu Ken with Hair	3849	$40.00	Ken
1981	Sunsational Malibu P.J.	1187	$25.00	P.J.
1981	Sunsational Malibu Skipper	1069	$15.00	Skipper
1982	All Star Ken	3553	$25.00	Ken

FAMILY & FRIENDS DOLLS

Listed by Year

YEAR	ITEM	NUMBER	VALUE	DOLL
1982	Beautiful Bride Tracy	4103	$65.00	Tracy
1982	Fashion Jeans Ken	5316	$50.00	Ken
1982	Pink and Pretty Christie	3555	$40.00	Christie
1982	Sunsational Malibu Christie	7745	$30.00	Christie
1982	Sunsational Malibu Ken	1088	$30.00	Ken
1982	Sunsational Malibu Ken (black)	3849	$30.00	Ken
1982	Sunsational Malibu P.J.	1187	$30.00	P.J.
1982	Sunsational Malibu Skipper	1069	$30.00	Skipper
1982	Super Sport Ken	5839	$25.00	Ken
1982	Western Ken	3600	$30.00	Ken
1982	Western Skipper	5029	$30.00	Skipper
1983	Barbie & Friends P.J.	4431	$40.00	P.J.
1983	Dream Date Ken	4077	$30.00	Ken
1983	Dream Date P.J.	5869	$30.00	P.J.
1983	Handsome Groom Todd	4253	$40.00	Todd
1983	Hawaiian Ken	7495	$40.00	Ken
1983	Horse Lovin' Ken	3600	$45.00	Ken
1983	Horse Lovin' Skipper	5029	$45.00	Skipper
1983	Sunsational Malibu Ken (Hispanic)	4971	$40.00	Ken
1983	Tracy Doll (Bridal)	4103	$40.00	Tracy
1984	Beach Time Ken	9103	$35.00	Ken
1984	Crystal Ken	4898	$25.00	Ken
1984	Crystal Ken (black)	9036	$35.00	Ken
1984	Great Shape Ken	7318	$25.00	Ken
1984	Great Shape Skipper	7414	$30.00	Skipper
1984	Sun Gold Malibu Ken	1088	$20.00	Ken
1984	Sun Gold Malibu Ken (Hispanic)	4971	$20.00	Ken
1984	Sun Gold Malibu P.J.	1187	$20.00	P.J.
1984	Sun Gold Malibu Skipper	1069	$20.00	Skipper
1984	Sweet Roses P.J.	7455	$45.00	P.J.
1985	Day-To-Night Ken	9019	$15.00	Ken
1985	Day-To-Night Ken (black)	9018	$15.00	Ken
1985	Hot Stuff Skipper	7927	$15.00	Skipper
1985	Music Lovin' Ken	2388	$45.00	Ken
1985	Music Lovin' Skipper	2854	$65.00	Skipper
1985	Sun Gold Malibu Ken (black)	3849	$20.00	Ken
1986	Dream Glow Ken	2250	$25.00	Ken
1986	Dream Glow Ken (black)	2421	$25.00	Ken
1986	Rocker Dana	1196	$30.00	Dana
1986	Rocker Dancin' Action Dana	3158	$35.00	Dana

FAMILY & FRIENDS DOLLS

Listed by Year

YEAR	ITEM	NUMBER	VALUE	DOLL
1986	Rocker Dancin' Action Dee Dee	3160	$35.00	Dee Dee
1986	Rocker Dancin' Action Diva	3159	$35.00	Diva
1986	Rocker Dee Dee	3160	$30.00	Dee Dee
1986	Rocker Derek	2428	$30.00	Derek
1986	Rocker Diva	2427	$30.00	Diva
1986	Rocker Hot Rockin' Derek	3173	$35.00	Derek
1986	Rocker Hot Rockin' Ken	3131	$35.00	Ken
1986	Rocker Ken	3131	$30.00	Ken
1986	Tropical Ken	1020	$12.00	Ken
1986	Tropical Ken (black)	1023	$15.00	Ken
1986	Tropical Miko	2056	$20.00	Miko
1986	Tropical Skipper	1021	$20.00	Skipper
1987	Doctor Ken	4118	$25.00	Ken
1987	Dr. Ken	4118	$25.00	Ken
1987	Jewel Secrets Ken	1719	$25.00	Ken
1987	Jewel Secrets Ken (black)	3232	$25.00	Ken
1987	Jewel Secrets Skipper	3133	$25.00	Skipper
1987	Jewel Secrets Whitney	3179	$45.00	Whitney
1987	Perfume Pretty Ken	4554	$30.00	Ken
1987	Perfume Pretty Ken (black)	4555	$30.00	Ken
1987	Rocker Dana (revised)	3158	$30.00	Dana
1987	Rocker Dee Dee (revised)	3160	$30.00	Dee Dee
1987	Rocker Derek (revised)	3137	$30.00	Derek
1987	Rocker Diva (revised)	3159	$30.00	Diva
1987	Rocker Ken (revised)	3131	$30.00	Ken
1988	California Dream Christie	4443	$25.00	Christie
1988	California Dream Ken	4441	$20.00	Ken
1988	California Dream Midge	4442	$20.00	Midge
1988	California Dream Teresa	5503	$20.00	Teresa
1988	Cheerleader Jazzie	3631	$25.00	Jazzie
1988	Cheerleader Teen Skipper	5893	$25.00	Skipper
1988	High School Chelsie	3698	$40.00	Chelsie
1988	High School Dude	3637	$40.00	Dude
1988	High School Jazzie	3635	$25.00	Jazzie
1988	High School Stacey	3636	$25.00	Stacey
1988	Island Fun Christie	4093	$25.00	Christie
1988	Island Fun Ken	4060	$35.00	Ken
1988	Island Fun Miko	4065	$25.00	Miko
1988	Island Fun Skipper	4064	$25.00	Skipper
1988	Island Fun Steven	4093	$25.00	Steven

FAMILY & FRIENDS DOLLS

Listed by Year

YEAR	ITEM	NUMBER	VALUE	DOLL
1988	Island Fun Teresa	4117	$25.00	Teresa
1988	Party Teen Doll	5899	N/A	Skipper
1988	Perfume Giving Ken	4554	N/A	Ken
1988	Perfume Giving Ken (black)	4555	N/A	Ken
1988	Perfume Pretty Whitney	4557	$40.00	Whitney
1988	Style Magic Whitney	1280	$25.00	Whitney
1988	Swim Suit Jazzie	3632	$25.00	Jazzie
1988	Teen Dance Jazzie	3634	$25.00	Jazzie
1988	Teen Sweetheart Skipper	4855	N/A	Skipper
1988	The Sensations Becky	4977	$25.00	Becky
1988	The Sensations Belinda	4976	$25.00	Belinda
1988	The Sensations Bopsy	4967	$25.00	Bopsy
1988	Workout Jazzie	3633	N/A	Jazzie
1988	Workout Teen Doll	5899	N/A	Skipper
1989	Animal Lovin' Ken	1351	$35.00	Ken
1989	Animal Lovin' Nikki	1352	$35.00	Nikki
1989	Beach Blast Christie	3253	$25.00	Christie
1989	Beach Blast Ken	3238	$15.00	Ken
1989	Beach Blast Miko	3244	$15.00	Miko
1989	Beach Blast Skipper	3242	$15.00	Skipper
1989	Beach Blast Steven	3251	$15.00	Steven
1989	Beach Blast Teresa	3249	$15.00	Teresa
1989	Cool Times Christie	3217	$20.00	Christie
1989	Cool Times Ken	3215	$20.00	Ken
1989	Cool Times Midge	3216	$20.00	Midge
1989	Cool Times Teresa	3218	$20.00	Teresa
1989	Dance Club Devon	3513	$35.00	Devon
1989	Dance Club Kayla	3512	$35.00	Kayla
1989	Dance Club Ken	3511	$35.00	Ken
1989	Homecoming Queen Skipper	1950	$45.00	Skipper
1989	Homecoming Queen Skipper (black)	2390	$45.00	Skipper
1989	My First Ken	1389	$15.00	Ken
1989	Pepsi Spirit Skipper	4867	$50.00	Skipper
1989	Style Magic Christie	1290	$25.00	Christie
1989	Style Magic Skipper	1915	$30.00	Skipper
1989	Sun Charm Ken	9934	$25.00	Ken
1989	Superstar Ken	1535	$35.00	Ken
1989	Superstar Ken (black)	1550	$35.00	Ken
1989	Teentime Courtney	1952	$25.00	Courtney
1989	Teentime Skipper	1951	N/A	Skipper

FAMILY & FRIENDS DOLLS

Listed by Year

YEAR	ITEM	NUMBER	VALUE	DOLL
1990	All Star Ken	9361	$20.00	Ken
1990	All Stars Midge	9360	$20.00	Midge
1990	All Stars Teresa	9353	$20.00	Teresa
1990	Barbie and the All Stars Christie	9352	$25.00	Christie
1990	Cool Tops Courtney	7079	$20.00	Courtney
1990	Cool Tops Kevin	9351	$20.00	Kevin
1990	Cool Tops Skipper	4989	$20.00	Skipper
1990	Cool Tops Skipper (black)	5441	$10.00	Skipper
1990	Dance Magic Ken	7081	$25.00	Ken
1990	Dance Magic Ken (black)	7082	$25.00	Ken
1990	Dream Date Kevin	9351	$25.00	Kevin
1990	Dream Date Skipper	4817	$30.00	Skipper
1990	Dream Date Skipper (black)	4849	$30.00	Skipper
1990	Flight Time Ken	9600	$40.00	Ken
1990	Ice Capades Ken	7375	$25.00	Ken
1990	My First Ken	9940	$15.00	Ken
1990	Scott Doll	1019	$45.00	Scott
1990	Sun Lovin' Malibu Jazzie	4088	$20.00	Jazzie
1990	The Beat Christie	2752	$25.00	Christie
1990	The Beat Midge	2754	$25.00	Midge
1990	Western Fun Ken	9934	$20.00	Ken
1990	Western Fun Nia	9933	$20.00	Nia
1990	Wet 'n Wild Christie	4121	$20.00	Christie
1990	Wet 'n Wild Ken	4104	$20.00	Ken
1990	Wet 'n Wild Kira	4120	$20.00	Kira
1990	Wet 'n Wild Skipper	4138	$20.00	Skipper
1990	Wet 'n Wild Steven	4137	$20.00	Steven
1990	Wet 'n Wild Teresa	4136	$20.00	Teresa
1990	Wet 'n Wild Whitney	4136	$80.00	Whitney
1991	30th Anniversary Ken	11581	$225.00	Ken
1991	All American Christie	9425	$25.00	Christie
1991	All American Ken	9424	$25.00	Ken
1991	All American Kira	9427	$25.00	Kira
1991	All American Teresa	9426	$25.00	Teresa
1991	Baby Sitter Courtney	9434	$10.00	Courtney
1991	Baby Sitter Kevin	9324	$10.00	Kevin
1991	Baby Sitter Skipper	9433	$10.00	Skipper
1991	Baby Sitter Skipper (black)	1599	$14.00	Skipper
1991	Beauty Pageant Skipper	9324	$35.00	Skipper
1991	Benetton Ken	9406	$50.00	Ken

BARBIE® OUTFITS

Listed Alphabetically

ITEM	NUMBER	YEAR	VALUE	SPECIALS
Wrap 'n Tie (blue)	1368	1980	2Xrtl	Beginner's Fashion
Wrap 'n Tie (red)	1369	1980	2Xrtl	Beginner's Fashion
Wrap, Snap, Tie	1370	1980	2Xrtl	Beginner's Fashion
Yellow and Blue Long Dress, Ruffle Neckline	7956	1985	Rtl	Twice as Nice Reversible
Yellow and Print Skirt, Printed Top	9011	1975	$45.00	Sears' Best Buys Exclusive
Yellow Go, The	1054	N/A	$225.00	Sears
Yellow Go, The	1816	1967	N/A	
Yellow Hat, Denim Pants and Vest, Shirt	12777	1995	Rtl	Western Fun Fashions
Yellow Jumper, Blouse, and Scarf	9162	1976	$40.00	Best Buys
Yellow Outfit	12625	1995	Rtl	Bead Fun Fashions
Yellow & Pink Two-Piece Bathing Suit	12648	1995	Rtl	Bath Paintin' Fashions
Yellow Sleep Set	3348	1973	$35.00	
Yellow Suit	9684	1976	$45.00	Sears' Best Buys Exclusived
Yellow Suit, Printed Halter	9909	1975	$45.00	Sears' Best Buys Exclusive
Yellow Top and Flared Leg Pants	12596	1995	Rtl	Picnic Pretty Fashions
Yellow-Mellow	1484	1969	$75.00	
Zig-Zag Bag, The	3428	1971	$110.00	
Zokko	1820	1968	$105.00	

Barbie® Outfits

Listed by Stock Number

Number	Item	Year	Value	Specials
0819	It's Cold Outside (brown)	1964	$150.00	
0819	It's Cold Outside (red)	1964	$140.00	
0820	Barbie in Mexico	1964	$225.00	Travel Outfits
0821	Barbie in Japan	1964	$375.00	Travel Outfits
0822	Barbie in Switzerland	1964	$200.00	Travel Outfits
0823	Barbie in Holland	1964	$200.00	Travel Outfits
0872	Cinderella	1964	$300.00	Little Theatre Costumes
0873	Guinevere	1964	$225.00	Little Theatre Costumes
0874	Barbie Arabian Nights	1964	$275.00	Little Theatre Costumes
0875	Drum Majorette	1964	$150.00	
0876	Cheerleader	1964	$175.00	
0880	Red Riding Hood and the Wolf	1964	$400.00	Little Theatre Costumes
0889	Candy Striper Volunteer	1964	$350.00	
0949	Stormy Weather	1964	$150.00	
0953	Baby Sits (layette)	1964	$325.00	
0957	Knitting Pretty (pink)	1963	$350.00	
0961	Evening Splendour (reissue)	1964	$175.00	
620	Gold Knit	N/A	$45.00	
870	Fashion Queen	1964	N/A	
911	Golden Girl	1959	$190.00	
912	Cotton Casual	1959	$125.00	
915	Peach Fleecy	1959	$105.00	
916	Commuter Set	1959	$850.00	
917	Apple Print Sheat	1959	$150.00	
918	Cruise Stripe Dress	1959	$150.00	
919	Fashion Undergarment	1959	$150.00	
921	Floral Petticoat	1959	$125.00	
931	Garden Party	1962	$125.00	
933	Movie Date	1962	$100.00	
933	Sophisticated Lady	1963	$250.00	
934	After Five	1962	$175.00	
937	Sorority Meeting	1962	$175.00	
939	Red Flare	1962	$100.00	
940	Mood for Music	1962	$150.00	
941	Tennis Anyone	1962	$75.00	
942	Icebreaker	1962	$75.00	
943	Fancy Free	1963	$100.00	
944	Masquerade	1963	$175.00	
945	Graduation	1963	$75.00	
946	Dinner At Eight	1963	$200.00	

BARBIE® OUTFITS

Listed by Stock Number

NUMBER	ITEM	YEAR	VALUE	SPECIALS
947	Bride's Dream	1963	$175.00	
948	Ski Queen	1963	$125.00	
949	Raincoat	1963	$65.00	
951	Senior Prom	1963	$175.00	
953	Baby-Sits	1962	$275.00	
954	Career Girl	1963	$275.00	
955	Swinging Easy	1963	$125.00	
956	Busy Morning	1963	$230.00	
957	Knitting Pretty (blue)	1963	$350.00	
957	Knitting Pretty (orange)	1963	$350.00	
958	Party Date	1963	$150.00	
959	Theatre Date	1963	$125.00	
961	Evening Splendour	1959	$200.00	
962	Barbie-Q Outfit	1959	$150.00	
963	Resort Set	1959	$130.00	
964	Gay Parisienne	1959	$2250.00	
965	Nighty-Negligee	1959	$125.00	
966	Plantation Bell Dress Set	1959	$300.00	
967	Picnic Set	1959	$300.00	
967	Picnic Set #2 (new hat, basket, fish)	1962	$250.00	
968	Roman Holiday Separates	1959	$3200.00	
969	Surburban Shopper	1959	$200.00	
971	Easter Parade	1959	$2600.00	
972	Wedding Day Set	1959	$1850.00	
973	Sweet Dreams	1959	$200.00	
975	Winter Holiday	1959	$175.00	
976	Sweater Girl	1959	$125.00	
977	Silken Flame	1960	$125.00	
978	Let's Dance	1960	$125.00	
979	Friday Nite Date	1960	$225.00	
981	Busy Gal	1960	$300.00	
982	Solo in the Spotlight	1960	$300.00	
983	Enchanted Evening	1960	$225.00	
984	American Airlines Stewardess	1961	$200.00	
985	Open Road	1961	$275.00	
986	Sheath Sensation	1961	$125.00	
987	Orange Blossom	1961	$95.00	
988	Singing in the Shower	1961	$75.00	
989	Ballerina	1961	$160.00	
991	Registered Nurse	1961	$150.00	

Barbie® Outfits

Listed by Stock Number

Number	Item	Year	Value	Specials
992	Golden Elegance	1963	$200.00	
1034	Hostess Set	1965	N/A	
1054	Yellow Go, The	N/A	$225.00	Sears
1055	Country Music	1971	$200.00	Fashions 'n Sound
1056	Festival Fashion	1971	$190.00	
1057	Groovin' Gauchos	1971	$170.00	
1061	Poodle Doodles	1972	$540.00	Put-Ons 'n Pets
1062	Kitty Kapers	1972	$545.00	Put-Ons 'n Pets
1063	Hot Togs	1972	$455.00	Put-Ons 'n Pets
1193	Perfectly Plaid	1971	N/A	Sears
1247	Strollin' in Style	1972	$40.00	
1368	Wrap 'n Tie (blue)	1980	2Xrtl	Beginner's Fashion
1369	Wrap 'n Tie (red)	1980	2Xrtl	Beginner's Fashion
1370	Wrap, Snap, Tie	1980	2Xrtl	Beginner's Fashion
1371	Slip On, Snap, Tie	1980	2Xrtl	Beginner's Fashion
1372	Slip On 'n Tie	1980	2Xrtl	Beginner's Fashion
1372	Slip On 'n Tie (red pants and top)	1981	2Xrtl	My First Barbie Fashions
1373	Wrap 'n Snap	1980	2Xrtl	Beginner's Fashion
1400	Pleasant Dreams	1980	2Xrtl	Barbie Fashion Favorites
1400	Pleasant Dreams	1981	2Xrtl	Fashion Favorites
1401	Summer Dance	1980	2Xrtl	Barbie Fashion Favorites
1402	Pink Perfection	1980	2Xrtl	Barbie Fashion Favorites
1403	Dressed to a "T"	1980	2Xrtl	Barbie Fashion Favorites
1412	Golden Glamour	1980	2Xrtl	Barbie & Ken Designer Original
1414	Evening Elegance	1980	2Xrtl	Barbie & Ken Designer Original
1416	Here Comes the Bride	1980	2Xrtl	Barbie & Ken Wedding Party
1417	Bridesmaid's Dream	1980	2Xrtl	Barbie & Ken Wedding Party
1427	Pink Champagne	1980	2Xrtl	Fashion Favorites
1428	Let's Dance	1980	2Xrtl	Fashion Favorites
1429	Fresh 'n Cool	1980	2Xrtl	Fashion Favorites
1430	Romantic Lady	1980	2Xrtl	Fashion Favorites
1440	Pink Sparkle	1967	$140.00	
1451	Tangerine Scene	1970	$45.00	
1452	Now Knit	1970	$60.00	
1453	Flower Wower	1970	$55.00	
1454	Loop Scoop	1970	$45.00	
1456	Dreamy Blues	1970	$50.00	
1457	City Sparklers	1970	$55.00	
1458	Gypsy Spirit	1970	$60.00	
1459	Great Coat	1970	$45.00	

Barbie® Outfits

Listed by Stock Number

Number	Item	Year	Value	Specials
5898	Candlelight Nights	1983	2Xrtl	Fashion Fun
7079	Ski Party	1984	2Xrtl	Designer Collection
7080	Horseback Ridin'	1984	2Xrtl	Designer Collection
7081	Bedtime Beauty	1984	2Xrtl	Designer Collection
7082	In the Spotlight	1984	2Xrtl	Designer Collection
7083	Picture in Plaid	1984	2Xrtl	Designer Collection
7092	Springtime Magic Fashion	1984	2Xrtl	Collectors' Series
7176	Bride	1976	$40.00	Get-Ups 'n Go
7216	Blue Magic	1984	2Xrtl	Spectacular Fashions
7217	Red Sizzle	1984	2Xrtl	Spectacular Fashions
7218	Dance Sensation	1984	2Xrtl	Spectacular Fashions
7219	In the Pink	1984	2Xrtl	Spectacular Fashions
7241	Indian Print Separates	1975	$35.00	Get-Ups 'n Go
7242	Casuals	1975	$40.00	Get-Ups 'n Go
7243	Olympic Warm-Ups	1975	$40.00	Get-Ups 'n Go
7244	Olympic Parade	1975	$40.00	Get-Ups 'n Go
7438	Silver Sensation Fashion	1984	2Xrtl	Collectors' Series III
7700	Doctor	1973	$50.00	Get-Ups 'n Go
7701	Ballerina	1973	$40.00	Get-Ups 'n Go
7702	Camping	1973	$35.00	
7703	United Airlines Stewardess	1973	$75.00	Get-Ups 'n Go
7787	Skiing	1974	$36.00	
7788	Beach	1974	$35.00	Get-Ups 'n Go
7839	Bride	1974	$40.00	Get-Ups 'n Go
7840	Blue Party Dress	1974	$35.00	
7841	Dreamy Designs for Dressy Dinners	N/A	$91.00	
7841	Pink Party Separates	1974	$35.00	Get-Ups 'n Go
7842	Tennis	1974	$45.00	Get-Ups 'n Go
7843	Salmon Party Dress	1974	$35.00	Get-Ups 'n Go
7843	Style Setter Gets Rave Review	N/A	$95.00	Get-Ups 'n Go
7859	Six to Midnight	N/A	$30.00	Get-Ups 'n Go
7910	Blue Jumpsuit, Gold Belt, and Collar	1985	Rtl	B Active Fashons
7911	Green Top, Yellow Pants	1985	Rtl	B Active Fashons
7912	White Top, Orange Shorts and Shoes	1985	Rtl	B Active Fashons
7913	Red & White Jogging Pants and Top, Sneakers	1985	Rtl	B Active Fashons
7914	White Long Shirt, Reg Leggings and Belt	1985	Rtl	B Active Fashions
7915	Fuschia Short Dress, Print Belt	1985	Rtl	B Active Fashions
7916	Blue/White Striped Top, Long Blue Skirt	1985	Rtl	B Active Fashons
7917	Fuschia Long Skirt and Top, Fuschia Shoes	1985	Rtl	B Active Fashions
7931	Red Evening Cape	1975	$40.00	Fashion Originals

BARBIE® OUTFITS

Listed by Stock Number

NUMBER	ITEM	YEAR	VALUE	SPECIALS
7932	Fashion Original	N/A	$75.00	
7933	Green Separates Set	1975	$34.00	Fashion Originals
7934	Rose Dress, Stole, Hat	1975	$35.00	Fashion Originals
7934	Rose Evening Gown and Jacket	1975	$40.00	Sears Fashion Originals
7950	Red Blouse, Black and White Skirt	1985	Rtl	Twice as Nice Reversible
7951	Red Hat, Red and White Coat	1985	Rtl	Twice as Nice Reversible
7952	Red Vest, Black Pants, White Shirt	1985	Rtl	Twice as Nice Reversible
7953	Fuschia/Blue Reversible Short Dress	1985	Rtl	Twice as Nice Reversible
7954	Striped Top, Yellow and Blue Vest and Skirt	1985	Rtl	Twice as Nice Reversible
7955	Green Pants, Yellow Top, Silver Jacket	1985	Rtl	Twice as Nice Reversible
7956	Yellow and Blue Long Dress, Ruffle Neckline	1985	Rtl	Twice as Nice Reversible
8620	Long Dark Printed Dress	1973	$40.00	
8621	Blue and White Checked Midi Suit	1973	$45.00	
8622	Red Pants, Sheer Overskirt, White Top	1973	$35.00	
8623	Wedding Gift	1973	$35.00	
8626	Shoes	1973	$20.00	
8670	Long Printed Skirt, Rose Blouse and Bag	1973	$65.00	Sew-Free Fashions
8680	Long Tricot Print	1973	$35.00	Best Buys
8681	Tan Shirt, Red Blouse	1973	$30.00	Best Buys
8682	Tan Coat, Fur Trim	1973	$30.00	Best Buys
8683	Long Printed Skirt, Yellow Blouse	1973	$35.00	Best Buys
8684	Long Off-White Dress	1973	$35.00	Best Buys
8685	Printed Pants, White Blouse, Yellow Weskit	1973	$35.00	Best Buys
8687	Pink Pants Suit	1973	$40.00	Best Buys
8688	Long Rose Dress, Black Net Coat	1973	$35.00	Best Buys
8689	Long Gold Skirt, White Blouse	1973	$35.00	Best Buys
8690	Robe and Nightgown	1973	$35.00	Best Buys
8691	Pants, Skirt, Hat, Blouse	1973	$30.00	Best Buys
8692	Blue Evening Gown	1973	$50.00	Best Buys
9006	Red Print Tricot	1975	$45.00	Sears' Best Buys Exclusive
9010	Red Plaid Pants and Jacket	1975	$45.00	Sears' Best Buys Exclusive
9011	Yellow and Print Skirt, Printed Top	1975	$45.00	Sears' Best Buys Exclusive
9042	Long Skirt, White Blouse	1975	$45.00	Sears Fashion Originals
9043	Regular Olympic Outfit	1975	$40.00	Sears Fashion Originals
9046	Printed Skirt, White Top	1975	$35.00	Fashion Originals
9047	Pants, Cape, Cap	1975	$55.00	Sears Fashion Originals
9048	Tweed Skirt, Blue Blouse	1975	$35.00	Fashion Originals
9048	Tweed Suit	1976	$40.00	Best Buys
9078	9-piece Red, White, Blue Outfit	1975	$50.00	Sears Fashion Originals
9081	Dress Designer	1985	Rtl	Day to Night Fashions

BARBIE® OUTFITS

Listed by Stock Number

NUMBER	ITEM	YEAR	VALUE	SPECIALS
9082	Dancer	1985	Rtl	Day to Night Fashions
9083	Business Executive	1985	Rtl	Day to Night Fashions
9084	TV News Reporter	1985	Rtl	
9085	Teachers	1985	Rtl	Day to Night Fashions
9143	Blue Skirt and Top, Red Top and Pants	1985	Rtl	Spectacular Fashions
9144	Light Blue Skirt Long and Short, Top, Jacket	1985	Rtl	Spectacular Fashions
9145	White Jacket, Skirt, Pants, Red Top and Skirt	1985	Rtl	Spectacular Fashions
9146	Red Top, Skirt, Pink Skirt, Top, 2-Tone Skirt	1985	Rtl	Spectacular Fashions
9151	Summer Gown	1976	$35.00	Get-Ups 'n Go
9152	Knit Ensemble	1976	$35.00	Get-Ups 'n Go
9152	Stripes Right for City Sights	N/A	$40.00	Get-Ups 'n Go
9153	Orange Checked Shirt, Top	1976	$40.00	Best Buys
9154	White Pants, Red Shirt	1976	$35.00	Best Buys
9155	Striped Dress	1976	$35.00	Best Buys
9156	Floral Printed Dress	1976	$35.00	Best Buys
9157	Rose Nightgown	1976	$30.00	Best Buys
9158	Red, White, Blue Dress	1976	$40.00	Best Buys
9160	Rose and White Printed Party Dress	1976	$25.00	Best Buys
9161	Blue Pants, Bandana Blouse	1976	$35.00	Best Buys
9162	Yellow Jumper, Blouse, and Scarf	1976	$40.00	Best Buys
9163	Underwear	1976	$30.00	Best Buys
9164	Red, White, Blue Print	1976	$40.00	Best Buys
9258	Collector Series IV	1985	Rtl	Oscar de La Renta
9259	Collector Series V	1985	Rtl	Oscar de La Renta
9260	Collector Series VI	1985	Rtl	Oscar de La Renta
9261	Collector Series VII	1985	Rtl	Oscar de La Renta
9263	Pink Swimsuit and Parasol	1985	Rtl	Fashion Playsets
9264	White Hat, Coat, Pink Scarf, Red Luggage	1985	Rtl	Fashion Playsets
9266	Fuschia Robe, Pink Towels, White Stand	1985	Rtl	Bath Fun Playset
9267	Vet Coat and Skirt with Dog	1985	Rtl	Fashion Playsets
9326	Sugar Plum Fairy	1976	$40.00	Ballerina Costumes
9327	Snowflake Fairy	1976	$40.00	Ballerina Costumes
9329	Princess Aurora	1976	$40.00	Ballerina Costumes
9571	Long Red Printed Dress	1976	$35.00	
9572	Gaucho Pants, Boots, Blouse	1976	$35.00	Best Buys
9573	Dress, Bag	1976	$35.00	Best Buys
9574	Pants, Shirt, Socks	1976	$30.00	Best Buys
9575	Long Printed Dress, Yellow Sleeves	1976	$35.00	Best Buys
9576	Checked Pants, Solid Shirt	1976	$40.00	
9577	Pink Party Dress	1976	$40.00	Best Buys

BARBIE® OUTFITS

Listed by Stock Number

NUMBER	ITEM	YEAR	VALUE	SPECIALS
9579	Blue Pants, Checked Top	1976	$35.00	Best Buys
9580	Long Yellow and Red Party Dress	1976	$35.00	Best Buys
9581	Pants, Jacket, Cap	1976	$40.00	
9582	Blue and Flame Short Party Dress	1976	$40.00	Best Buys
9594	Pink Evening Gown	1976	$40.00	Get-Ups 'n Go
9595	Coral Evening Gown	1976	$35.00	Get-Ups 'n Go
9650	Ballerina Costume	1975	$45.00	Sears
9650	Mix 'n Match Set	1976	$40.00	Sears
9650	Red Evening Gown and Cape	1976	$45.00	Sears
9650	Red Palazzo Pants, Gold Halter	1976	$45.00	Sears
9670	8-piece Coordinated Set	1976	$45.00	Sears
9682	Black and Rose Nightgown	1976	$45.00	Sears' Best Buys Exclusive
9683	White with Navy Stripes Dress	1976	$45.00	Sears' Best Buys Exclusive
9684	Yellow Suit	1976	$45.00	Sears' Best Buys Exclusived
9685	Blue Pants, Yellow Top	1976	$40.00	Sears' Best Buys Exclusive
9686	Long Blue and White Printed Dress	1976	$40.00	
9687	Long Red and White Dress	1976	$35.00	
9907	Blue Denim Dress and Hat	1975	$40.00	Sears' Best Buys Exclusive
9908	Pink Baby Dolls	1975	$40.00	Sears' Best Buys Exclusive
9909	Yellow Suit, Printed Halter	1975	$45.00	Sears' Best Buys Exclusive
10773	Teacher, Firefighter, Veterinarian Outfits	1995	Rtl	Caring Careers Fashion
11558	Purple Locket Surprise Fashions	1994	$5.00	Locket Surprise Fashions
11559	Peach Locket Surprise Fashions	1994	$5.00	Locket Surprise Fashions
11560	Aqua Locket Surprise Fashions	1994	$5.00	Locket Surprise Fashions
11935	Long Skirt and Top	1994	$4.00	Fashion Forms Fashions
11936	Dress and Jacket	1994	$4.00	Fashion Forms Fashions
11937	Dress and Shoulder Bag	1994	$4.00	Fashion Forms Fashions
11938	Mini and Jacket	1994	$4.00	Fashion Forms Fashions
12183	Jewel & Glitter Fashions Barbie	1994	$5.00	Jewel & Glitter
12437	Print Skirt and Yellow Halter Top	1995	Rtl	Make Up Pretty Fashions
12438	Pink Shorts and Tank with Print Jacket	1995	Rtl	Make Up Pretty Fashions
12439	Striped Pants, Purple Top	1995	Rtl	Make Up Pretty Fashions
12440	Striped Skirt, Green Top	1995	Rtl	Make Up Pretty Fashions
12594	Pink and White Pants and Halter Top	1995	Rtl	Picnic Pretty Fashions
12595	Purple Shorts and Purple Jacket	1995	Rtl	Picnic Pretty Fashions
12596	Yellow Top and Flared Leg Pants	1995	Rtl	Picnic Pretty Fashions
12597	Green Skirt, White & Green Blouse	1995	Rtl	Picnic Pretty Fashions
12600	Princess	1995	Rtl	My First Fashions
12601	Ballerina	1995	Rtl	My First Fashions
12602	Angel	1995	Rtl	My First Fashions

BARBIE® OUTFITS

Listed by Stock Number

NUMBER	ITEM	YEAR	VALUE	SPECIALS
12603	Ice Skater	1995	Rtl	My First Fashions
12623	Pink Outfit	1995	Rtl	Bead Fun Fashions
12624	Green Outfit	1995	Rtl	Bead Fun Fashions
12625	Yellow Outfit	1995	Rtl	Bead Fun Fashions
12626	Blue Outfit	1995	Rtl	Bead Fun Fashions
12628	Pink Shorts & White Top and Pants	1995	Rtl	Sponge 'n Print Fashions
12629	Blue Jacket & White Short Outfit	1995	Rtl	Sponge 'n Print Fashions
12630	White Outfit & Pink Vest	1995	Rtl	Sponge 'n Print Fashions
12631	White Jacket & Top and Purple Shorts	1995	Rtl	Sponge 'n Print Fashions
12634	Red Dress & Black Vest	1995	Rtl	Paint the Dots Fashion
12635	Black Pants & White Top	1995	Rtl	Paint the Dots Fashion
12636	Green Dress & Black Top	1995	Rtl	Paint the Dots Fashion
12637	Black Shorts, Orange Jacket, White Top	1995	Rtl	Paint the Dots Fashion
12645	Blue Bathing Suit	1995	Rtl	Bath Paintin' Fashions
12646	Blue & Orange One Piece Bathing Suit	1995	Rtl	Bath Paintin' Fashions
12647	Pink & Green Two Piece Bathing Suit	1995	Rtl	Bath Paintin' Fashions
12648	Yellow & Pink Two-Piece Bathing Suit	1995	Rtl	Bath Paintin' Fashions
12776	Denim Shorts, Bandana Print Halter	1995	Rtl	Western Fun Fashions
12777	Yellow Hat, Denim Pants and Vest, Shirt	1995	Rtl	Western Fun Fashions
12778	Bandana Skirt and Top, Red Cowboy Hat	1995	Rtl	Western Fun Fashions
12779	Denim Dress, Pink Bandana, Print Jacket	1995	Rtl	Western Fun Fashions
13017	Red Jumper, Blue and White Striped Top	1995	Rtl	Yacht Club Fashions
13018	Blue Shorts, White Top, Yellow Jacket	1995	Rtl	Yacht Club Fashions
13019	White Pants, Red Belt, Blue and White Halter	1995	Rtl	Yacht Club Fashions
13020	Red and White Swimsuit, Red and Blue Jacket	1995	Rtl	Yacht Club Fashions
13024	Pink Ballgown	1995	Rtl	Fantasy Evening Fashions
13025	Pink & White Ballgown	1995	Rtl	Fantasy Evening Fashions
13203	Gold Ballgown	1995	Rtl	Fantasy Evening Fashions

BARBIE® OUTFITS

Listed by Year

YEAR	ITEM	NUMBER	VALUE	SPECIALS
1959	Apple Print Sheat	917	$150.00	
1959	Barbie-Q Outfit	962	$150.00	
1959	Commuter Set	916	$850.00	
1959	Cotton Casual	912	$125.00	
1959	Cruise Stripe Dress	918	$150.00	
1959	Easter Parade	971	$2600.00	
1959	Evening Splendour	961	$200.00	
1959	Fashion Undergarment	919	$150.00	
1959	Floral Petticoat	921	$125.00	
1959	Gay Parisienne	964	$2250.00	
1959	Golden Girl	911	$190.00	
1959	Nighty-Negligee	965	$125.00	
1959	Peach Fleecy	915	$105.00	
1959	Picnic Set	967	$300.00	
1959	Plantation Bell Dress Set	966	$300.00	
1959	Resort Set	963	$130.00	
1959	Roman Holiday Separates	968	$3200.00	
1959	Surburban Shopper	969	$200.00	
1959	Sweater Girl	976	$125.00	
1959	Sweet Dreams	973	$200.00	
1959	Wedding Day Set	972	$1850.00	
1959	Winter Holiday	975	$175.00	
1960	Busy Gal	981	$300.00	
1960	Enchanted Evening	983	$225.00	
1960	Friday Nite Date	979	$225.00	
1960	Let's Dance	978	$125.00	
1960	Silken Flame	977	$125.00	
1960	Solo in the Spotlight	982	$300.00	
1961	American Airlines Stewardess	984	$200.00	
1961	Ballerina	989	$160.00	
1961	Open Road	985	$275.00	
1961	Orange Blossom	987	$95.00	
1961	Registered Nurse	991	$150.00	
1961	Sheath Sensation	986	$125.00	
1961	Singing in the Shower	988	$75.00	
1962	Accessory Pack	Pak	N/A	
1962	After Five	934	$175.00	
1962	Apron and Utensils	Pak	N/A	
1962	Baby-Sits	953	$275.00	
1962	Bell Dress	Pak	N/A	

Barbie® Outfits

Listed by Year

Year	Item	Number	Value	Specials
1962	Cardigan	Pak	N/A	
1962	Fur Stole with Bag	Pak	N/A	
1962	Garden Party	931	$125.00	
1962	Gathered Skirt	Pak	N/A	
1962	Helanca Swimsuit	Pak	N/A	
1962	Icebreaker	942	$75.00	
1962	Lingerie Pack	Pak	N/A	
1962	Mood for Music	940	$150.00	
1962	Movie Date	933	$100.00	
1962	Picnic Set #2 (new hat, basket, fish)	967	$250.00	
1962	Plain Blouse and Purse	Pak	N/A	
1962	Purse Pack	Pak	N/A	
1962	Red Flare	939	$100.00	
1962	Scoop Neck Playsuit	Pak	N/A	
1962	Sheath Skirt and Telephone	Pak	N/A	
1962	Sheath with Gold Buttons	Pak	N/A	
1962	Silk Sheath	Pak	N/A	
1962	Slacks	Pak	N/A	
1962	Slip, Pant, Bra	Pak	N/A	
1962	Sorority Meeting	937	$175.00	
1962	Square Neck Sweater	Pak	N/A	
1962	Tee Shirt and Shorts	Pak	N/A	
1962	Tennis Anyone	941	$75.00	
1962	Two-Piece Pajamas	Pak	N/A	
1963	Bride's Dream	947	$175.00	
1963	Busy Morning	956	$230.00	
1963	Career Girl	954	$275.00	
1963	Dinner At Eight	946	$200.00	
1963	Fancy Free	943	$100.00	
1963	Full Satin Evening Skirt	Pak	N/A	
1963	Fur Hat/Bag	Pak	N/A	
1963	Gold Lamé Sheath	Pak	N/A	
1963	Golden Elegance	992	$200.00	
1963	Graduation	945	$75.00	
1963	Jeans	Pak	N/A	
1963	Knit Blouse	Pak	N/A	
1963	Knit Full Evening Skirt	Pak	N/A	
1963	Knit Sheath Dress with Fringed Collar	Pak	N/A	
1963	Knit Sheath Skirt and Sash	Pak	N/A	
1963	Knit Shorts and Top	Pak	N/A	

This is the porcelain re-creation of Barbie doll wearing the Gay Parisienne outfit issued in 1959. This doll was issued in 1991. She was made in blonde, brunette, and Titian hair.

The brunette Snow Princess was a convention special from the 1994 Orlando Convention at Disney World. This doll was limited to 285. The blonde Snow Princess is the first in the Enchanted Season series. This was available through mail order in 1994 and 1995.

KEN® OUTFITS

Listed Alphabetically

ITEM	YEAR	NUMBER	VALUE	SPECIALS
Accessory Pack	1962	Pak	N/A	
American Airlines Captain	1964	0779	$210.00	
Argyle Pants, Knit Top, Red and Black Pants	1974	7707	N/A	
Army and Air Force	1963	797	$130.00	
At Ease	1964	Pak	N/A	
Baseball	1976	N/A	N/A	
Beach Beat	1972	3384	N/A	
Belted Coat	1975	7227	N/A	
Best Foot Forward	1964	Pak	N/A	
Black Pants	1985	9116	N/A	Twice as Nice Reversible
Black Pants, Polka Dotted Shirt	1975	9002	N/A	
Blazer	1962	Pak	N/A	
Blue Jacket & Clear Case	1995	13570	Rtl	On the Go Fashions
Blue Pants, Blue and White Jacket	1985	9118	N/A	Twice as Nice Reversible
Blue Pants, Printed Shirt	1976	9696	N/A	
Blue Pants, White Shirt, Blue and Red Vest	1985	9914	N/A	Twice as Nice Reversible
Blue Police Uniform with Hat	1995	12609	Rtl	Cool Looks Fashion
Blue Shirt & Pouch	1995	13569	Rtl	On the Go Fashions
Blueprint for Success	1981	1947	N/A	Ken Fashion Favorites
Bold Gold	1970	1436	$40.00	
Boxing Outfit	1963	Pak	N/A	
Breakfast at 7	1969	1428	$40.00	
Bridegroom (blue and black)	1974	7836	N/A	
Brown on Brown	1972	1718	$70.00	
Brown Pants, Argyle Shirt	1974	7758	N/A	
Brown Slacks	1962	Pak	N/A	
Brown Suit	1974	7838	N/A	
Business Appointment	1966	1424	$975.00	
Business Suit	1975	7246	N/A	
Camping	1973	7706	N/A	
Campus Corduroys	1964	1410	$120.00	
Campus Hero	1961	0770	$130.00	
Cardigan Sweater	1963	Pak	N/A	
Casual All-Stars	1970	1436	N/A	
Casual Cords	1972	1717	$60.00	
Casual Scene	1971	1472	$40.00	
Casual Suit	1976	9167	N/A	
Casuals (striped shirt)	1964	0782	$75.00	
Casuals (yellow shirt)	1962	782	$75.00	
Checked Pants, Denim Jacket	1975	9904	N/A	Best Buys

KEN® OUTFITS

Listed Alphabetically

ITEM	YEAR	NUMBER	VALUE	SPECIALS
Pants, Tee Shirt, Cap	1976	9129	N/A	
Pants, Tee Shirt, Hat	1976	9132	N/A	
Party Fun	1964	Pak	N/A	
Pattern Printed Shirt	1962	Pak	N/A	
Pepsi Outfit	1974	7761	N/A	
Pilot Uniform	1967	1427	N/A	
Pink, Green, Black Top, Shorts, Surf Board	1995	12607	Rtl	Cool Looks Fashions
Plaid Jacket & Brown Cast	1995	13567	Rtl	On the Go Fashions
Plaid Pants, Black Jacket	1975	9047	N/A	
Play Ball	1963	792	$80.00	
Polo Shirt	1962	Pak	N/A	
Prince, The	1964	0772	$260.00	
Rain or Shine	1984	4888	N/A	Twice as Nice Fashions
Rally Day	1962	788	$65.00	
Rally Gear	1969	1429	$65.00	
Red and White Pajamas	1975	9903	N/A	
Red Pants and Jacket	1974	7762	N/A	
Red Pants, Beige Shirt	1975	7226	N/A	
Red Pants, Plaid Shirt	1974	7759	N/A	
Red Pants, Printed Shirt	1976	9698	N/A	
Red Printed Shirt, Blue Pants	1974	7707	N/A	
Red Shirt, Red and White Pants	1976	9699	N/A	
Red Vest	1962	Pak	N/A	
Red, White, and Wild	1972	1829	$30.00	
Red, White, Blue Shorts and Shirt/Soccer Official	1995	12608	Rtl	Cool Looks Fashions
Red & White Striped Shirt, Red/White Pants	1985	9115	N/A	Twice as Nice Reversible
Roller Skate Date	1964	1405	$75.00	
Roller Skate Date (cap omitted, slacks added)	1965	1405	$70.00	
Rovin' Reporter	1965	1417	$250.00	
Running Start	1981	1404	N/A	Ken Fashion Favorites
Sailor	1963	796	$100.00	
Saturday Date	1961	786	$75.00	
Sea Scene	1971	1449	$45.00	
Seein' the Sights	1966	1421	$240.00	
Sewn Sweater	1962	Pak	N/A	
Ship-Shape	1984	4885	N/A	Twice as Nice Fashions
Shoe Ins	1970	N/A	N/A	
Shoes	1973	8627	N/A	
Shoes for Sport	1964	Pak	N/A	
Simply Dashing	1984	7084	N/A	Designer Collection

KEN® OUTFITS

Listed Alphabetically

ITEM	YEAR	NUMBER	VALUE	SPECIALS
Ski Champion	1963	798	$60.00	
Skiing Scene	1971	1438	$75.00	Get-Ups 'n Go
Skin Diver	1964	3772	N/A	Sears
Slacks Are Back	1970	N/A	N/A	
Sleeper Set (blue)	1964	0781	$60.00	
Sleeper Set (long sleeves)	1961	781	$40.00	
Sleeper Set (short sleeves)	1961	781	$45.00	
Snow Bound	1981	1948	N/A	Ken Fashion Favorites
Soda Date	1964	Pak	N/A	
Solid Color Sport Shirt	1962	Pak	N/A	
Special Date	1964	1401	$160.00	
Sport Shirt	1961	783	$40.00	
Sportsman	1964	Pak	N/A	
Striped Sweater & Nap Sack	1995	13568	N/A	On the Go Fashions
Striped Tank Top, Denims	1976	9697	N/A	
Suede Scene	1971	1439	$55.00	
Suit, Blue Pants, Red and Blue Jacket	1974	7763	N/A	
Suited for the Groom	1980	1418	N/A	Barbie & Ken Wedding Party
Suited for the Groom	1983	5744	N/A	Wedding of the Year
Summer Job	1966	1422	$160.00	
Sun Fun	1970	N/A	N/A	
Surf's Up	1971	1248	N/A	
Sweat Shirt	1963	Pak	N/A	
Tan Pants, Red and Tan Striped Shirt	1985	9117	N/A	Twice as Nice Reversible
Tennis	1974	7837	N/A	
Tennis Everyone	1980	1405	N/A	Ken Fashion Favorites
Terry Togs	1961	784	$40.00	
Time for Tennis	1962	790	$65.00	
Time to Turn In	1966	1418	$90.00	
Top It Off	1964	Pak	N/A	
Touchdown	1963	799	$65.00	
Town Turtle	1969	1430	$40.00	
Tuxedo	1961	787	$150.00	
Tuxedo	1995	13026	N/A	Fantasy Evening Fashions
TV Sports Reporter	1985	9086	N/A	Day to Night Fashions
TV's Good Tonight	1966	1419	$140.00	
Tweed Suit	1975	9048	N/A	
United Airlines Pilot Outfit	1973	7707	N/A	
V.I.P. Scene	1971	1473	$50.00	
Victory Dance	1964	1411	$155.00	

KEN® OUTFITS

Listed Alphabetically

ITEM	YEAR	NUMBER	VALUE	SPECIALS
Way-Out West	1972	1720	$30.00	
Well Suited	1980	1407	N/A	Ken Fashion Favorites
Western Shirt, Jeans, Hat, Vest, Bandana	1995	12606	N/A	Cool Looks Fashions
Western Winner	1972	3377	N/A	
White Dress Shirt	1962	Pak	N/A	
White Is Right	1964	Pak	N/A	
White Pants, Red and White Printed Shirt	1973	8615	N/A	
White Shorts and Tank, Blue Shirt	1985	9113	N/A	Twice as Nice Reversible
Wide Awake Stripes	1972	3377	N/A	
Windbreaker	1962	Pak	N/A	
Yachtsman, The (no cap)	1962	789	$125.00	
Yatchsman, The (with cap)	1964	789	$130.00	
Yellow and Blue Set	1976	9130	N/A	

KEN® OUTFITS

Listed by Stock Number

NUMBER	ITEM	YEAR	VALUE	SPECIALS
0770	Campus Hero	1961	$130.00	
0772	Prince, The	1964	$260.00	
0773	King Arthur	1964	$200.00	
0774	Ken Arabian Nights	1964	$130.00	
0775	Drum Major	1964	$140.00	
0776	Ken in Switzerland	1964	$175.00	
0777	Ken in Holland	1964	$145.00	
0778	Ken in Mexico	1964	$170.00	
0779	American Airlines Captain	1964	$210.00	
780	In Training	1961	$45.00	
0781	Sleeper Set (blue)	1964	$60.00	
781	Sleeper Set (long sleeves)	1961	$40.00	
781	Sleeper Set (short sleeves)	1961	$45.00	
0782	Casuals (striped shirt)	1964	$75.00	
782	Casuals (yellow shirt)	1962	$75.00	
783	Sport Shirt	1961	$40.00	
784	Terry Togs	1961	$40.00	
785	Dreamboat	1961	$80.00	
786	Saturday Date	1961	$75.00	
787	Tuxedo	1961	$150.00	
788	Rally Day	1962	$65.00	
789	Yachtsman, The (no cap)	1962	$125.00	
789	Yatchsman, The (with cap)	1964	$130.00	
790	Time for Tennis	1962	$65.00	
791	Fun on Ice	1963	$75.00	
792	Play Ball	1963	$80.00	
793	Dr. Ken	1963	$115.00	
794	Masquerade	1963	$70.00	
795	Graduation	1963	$30.00	
796	Sailor	1963	$100.00	
797	Army and Air Force	1963	$130.00	
798	Ski Champion	1963	$60.00	
799	Touchdown	1963	$65.00	
1248	Surf's Up	1971	N/A	
1400	Country Clubbin'	1964	$110.00	
1401	Special Date	1964	$160.00	
1403	Going Bowling	1964	$60.00	
1404	Ken in Hawaii	1964	$125.00	
1404	Running Start	1981	N/A	Ken Fashion Favorites
1405	Roller Skate Date	1964	$75.00	

KEN® OUTFITS

Listed by Stock Number

Number	Item	Year	Value	Specials
1405	Roller Skate Date (cap omitted, slacks added)	1965	$70.00	
1405	Tennis Everyone	1980	N/A	Ken Fashion Favorites
1406	Ken Skin Diver	1964	$45.00	
1406	Outdoor Man	1980	N/A	Ken Fashion Favorites
1407	Fountain Boy	1964	$165.00	
1407	Well Suited	1980	N/A	Ken Fashion Favorites
1408	Fraternity Metting	1964	$70.00	
1409	Goin' Huntin'	1964	$85.00	
1410	Campus Corduroys	1964	$120.00	
1411	Victory Dance	1964	$155.00	
1412	Hiking Holiday	1965	$185.00	
1413	Golden Glamour	1980	N/A	Barbie & Ken Designer Original
1413	Off to Bed	1965	$130.00	
1414	Holiday	1965	$155.00	
1415	Evening Elegance	1980	N/A	Barbie & Ken Designer Original
1415	Mr. Astronaut	1965	$725.00	
1416	College Student	1965	$400.00	
1417	Rovin' Reporter	1965	$250.00	
1418	Suited for the Groom	1980	N/A	Barbie & Ken Wedding Party
1418	Time to Turn In	1966	$90.00	
1419	TV's Good Tonight	1966	$140.00	
1420	Jazz Concert	1966	$260.00	
1421	Seein' the Sights	1966	$240.00	
1422	Summer Job	1966	$160.00	
1423	Ken A Go Go	1966	$450.00	
1424	Business Appointment	1966	$975.00	
1426	Here Comes the Groom	1965	$800.00	
1427	Mountain Hike	1966	$180.00	
1427	Pilot Uniform	1967	N/A	
1428	Breakfast at 7	1969	$40.00	
1429	Rally Gear	1969	$65.00	
1430	Town Turtle	1969	$40.00	
1431	Guruvy Formal	1969	$50.00	
1436	Bold Gold	1970	$40.00	
1436	Casual All-Stars	1970	N/A	
1438	Skiing Scene	1971	$75.00	Get-Ups 'n Go
1439	Suede Scene	1971	$55.00	
1449	Sea Scene	1971	$45.00	
1472	Casual Scene	1971	$40.00	
1473	V.I.P. Scene	1971	$50.00	

KEN® OUTFITS

Listed by Stock Number

Number	Item	Year	Value	Specials
1496	Night Scene	1971	$65.00	
1595	Fabulous Formal Set	1969	N/A	
1717	Casual Cords	1972	$60.00	
1718	Brown on Brown	1972	$70.00	
1719	Midnight Blues	1972	$120.00	
1720	Way-Out West	1972	$30.00	
1828	Mod Madras	1972	$90.00	
1829	Red, White, and Wild	1972	$30.00	
1947	Blueprint for Success	1981	N/A	Ken Fashion Favorites
1948	Snow Bound	1981	N/A	Ken Fashion Favorites
1949	Classic Cowboy	1981	N/A	Ken Fashion Favorites
1956	Paint the Town Red	1981	N/A	Barbie & Ken Designer Original
3377	Cook 'n Casual	1972	N/A	
3377	Western Winner	1972	N/A	
3377	Wide Awake Stripes	1972	N/A	
3384	Beach Beat	1972	N/A	
3772	Skin Diver	1964	N/A	Sears
3797	Dandy Lines	1982	N/A	Barbie & Ken Designer Original
4276	Fun at McDonalds	1983	N/A	Fashion Classics
4885	Ship-Shape	1984	N/A	Twice as Nice Fashions
4886	Double Play	1984	N/A	Twice as Nice Fashions
4887	Doublevested	1984	N/A	Twice as Nice Fashions
4888	Rain or Shine	1984	N/A	Twice as Nice Fashions
4889	Handsome Pair	1984	N/A	Twice as Nice Fashions
4890	Dashing Duo	1984	N/A	Twice as Nice Fashions
5651	Date Night	1983	N/A	Designer Collection
5744	Suited for the Groom	1983	N/A	Wedding of the Year
5819	Go-Anywhere Gear	1983	N/A	Fashion Classics
5820	Country Flair	1983	N/A	Fashion Classics
5821	Keeping in Shape	1983	N/A	Fashion Classics
5822	Cool 'n Casual	1983	N/A	Fashion Classics
5823	Cool Captain	1983	N/A	Fashion Classics
5824	Date with Barbie Doll	1983	N/A	Fashion Classics
5833	Country Gentlemen	1983	N/A	Designer Collection
7084	Simply Dashing	1984	N/A	Designer Collection
7224	Checked Pants, Red Sweater	1975	N/A	
7225	Jeans Suit, Red Printed Yoke	1975	N/A	
7226	Red Pants, Beige Shirt	1975	N/A	
7227	Belted Coat	1975	N/A	
7229	Navy Pants, Plaid Jacket, Red Dickey	1975	N/A	

KEN® OUTFITS

Listed by Stock Number

NUMBER	ITEM	YEAR	VALUE	SPECIALS
7245	Olympic Outfit	1975	N/A	
7246	Business Suit	1975	N/A	
7247	Olympic Hockey	1975	N/A	
7705	Doctor Outfit	1973	N/A	
7706	Camping	1973	N/A	
7707	Argyle Pants, Knit Top, Red and Black Pants	1974	N/A	
7707	Red Printed Shirt, Blue Pants	1974	N/A	
7707	United Airlines Pilot Outfit	1973	N/A	
7758	Brown Pants, Argyle Shirt	1974	N/A	
7759	Red Pants, Plaid Shirt	1974	N/A	
7760	Green Pants, Hawaiian Shirt	1974	N/A	
7761	Pepsi Outfit	1974	N/A	
7762	Red Pants and Jacket	1974	N/A	
7763	Suit, Blue Pants, Red and Blue Jacket	1974	N/A	
7836	Bridegroom (blue and black)	1974	N/A	
7837	Tennis	1974	N/A	
7838	Brown Suit	1974	N/A	
8615	White Pants, Red and White Printed Shirt	1973	N/A	
8616	Navy Slacks, Yellow and Navy 73 on Sweater	1973	N/A	
8617	Light Brown Pants and Jacket, Gold Dickey	1973	N/A	
8618	Denim Suit with Red Plaid Trim	1973	N/A	
8627	Shoes	1973	N/A	
9001	Dark Pants, Printed Shirt	1975	N/A	
9002	Black Pants, Polka Dotted Shirt	1975	N/A	
9046	Light Pants, Jacket with Printed Yoke	1975	N/A	
9047	Plaid Pants, Black Jacket	1975	N/A	
9048	Tweed Suit	1975	N/A	
9086	TV Sports Reporter	1985	N/A	Day to Night Fashions
9113	White Shorts and Tank, Blue Shirt	1985	N/A	Twice as Nice Reversible
9115	Red & White Striped Shirt, Red/White Pants	1985	N/A	Twice as Nice Reversible
9116	Black Pants	1985	N/A	Twice as Nice Reversible
9117	Tan Pants, Red and Tan Striped Shirt	1985	N/A	Twice as Nice Reversible
9118	Blue Pants, Blue and White Jacket	1985	N/A	Twice as Nice Reversible
9127	Pants, Jacket Shirt	1976	N/A	
9128	Pants, Jacket, Scarf	1976	N/A	
9129	Pants, Tee Shirt, Cap	1976	N/A	
9130	Yellow and Blue Set	1976	N/A	
9131	Pants, Shirt, Cap	1976	N/A	
9132	Pants, Tee Shirt, Hat	1976	N/A	
9167	Casual Suit	1976	N/A	

KEN® OUTFITS

Listed by Stock Number

NUMBER	ITEM	YEAR	VALUE	SPECIALS
9596	Groom	1976	N/A	
9696	Blue Pants, Printed Shirt	1976	N/A	
9697	Striped Tank Top, Denims	1976	N/A	
9698	Red Pants, Printed Shirt	1976	N/A	
9699	Red Shirt, Red and White Pants	1976	N/A	
9903	Red and White Pajamas	1975	N/A	
9904	Checked Pants, Denim Jacket	1975	N/A	Best Buys
9914	Blue Pants, White Shirt, Blue and Red Vest	1985	N/A	Twice as Nice Reversible
12606	Western Shirt, Jeans, Hat, Vest, Bandana	1995	N/A	Cool Looks Fashions
12607	Pink, Green, Black Top, Shorts, Surf Board	1995	N/A	Cool Looks Fashions
12608	Red, White, Blue Shorts & Shirt/Soccer Official	1995	N/A	Cool Looks Fashions
12609	Blue Police Uniform with Hat	1995	N/A	Cool Looks Fashion
13026	Tuxedo	1995	N/A	Fantasy Evening Fashions
13567	Plaid Jacket & Brown Cast	1995	N/A	On the Go Fashions
13568	Striped Sweater & Nap Sack	1995	N/A	On the Go Fashions
13569	Blue Shirt & Pouch	1995	N/A	On the Go Fashions
13570	Blue Jacket & Clear Case	1995	N/A	On the Go Fashions

KEN® OUTFITS

Listed by Year

YEAR	ITEM	NUMBER	VALUE	SPECIALS
1961	Campus Hero	0770	$130.00	
1961	Dreamboat	785	$80.00	
1961	In Training	780	$45.00	
1961	Saturday Date	786	$75.00	
1961	Sleeper Set (long sleeves)	781	$40.00	
1961	Sleeper Set (short sleeves)	781	$45.00	
1961	Sport Shirt	783	$40.00	
1961	Terry Togs	784	$40.00	
1961	Tuxedo	787	$150.00	
1962	Accessory Pack	Pak	N/A	
1962	Blazer	Pak	N/A	
1962	Brown Slacks	Pak	N/A	
1962	Casuals (yellow shirt)	782	$75.00	
1962	Cord Slacks	Pak	N/A	
1962	Corduroy Jacket	Pak	N/A	
1962	Gray Slacks	Pak	N/A	
1962	Pattern Printed Shirt	Pak	N/A	
1962	Polo Shirt	Pak	N/A	
1962	Rally Day	788	$65.00	
1962	Red Vest	Pak	N/A	
1962	Sewn Sweater	Pak	N/A	
1962	Solid Color Sport Shirt	Pak	N/A	
1962	Time for Tennis	790	$65.00	
1962	White Dress Shirt	Pak	N/A	
1962	Windbreaker	Pak	N/A	
1962	Yachtsman, The (no cap)	789	$125.00	
1963	Army and Air Force	797	$130.00	
1963	Boxing Outfit	Pak	N/A	
1963	Cardigan Sweater	Pak	N/A	
1963	Dr. Ken	793	$115.00	
1963	Fun on Ice	791	$75.00	
1963	Graduation	795	$30.00	
1963	Hunting Outfit	Pak	N/A	
1963	Jeans	Pak	N/A	
1963	Masquerade	794	$70.00	
1963	Play Ball	792	$80.00	
1963	Sailor	796	$100.00	
1963	Ski Champion	798	$60.00	
1963	Sweat Shirt	Pak	N/A	
1963	Touchdown	799	$65.00	

KEN® OUTFITS

Listed by Year

YEAR	ITEM	NUMBER	VALUE	SPECIALS
1964	American Airlines Captain	0779	$210.00	
1964	At Ease	Pak	N/A	
1964	Best Foot Forward	Pak	N/A	
1964	Campus Corduroys	1410	$120.00	
1964	Casuals (striped shirt)	0782	$75.00	
1964	Cheerful Chef	Pak	N/A	
1964	Country Clubbin'	1400	$110.00	
1964	Dr. Ken's Kit	Pak	N/A	
1964	Drum Major	0775	$140.00	
1964	Fountain Boy	1407	$165.00	
1964	Fraternity Metting	1408	$70.00	
1964	Goin' Huntin'	1409	$85.00	
1964	Going Bowling	1403	$60.00	
1964	Ken Arabian Nights	0774	$130.00	
1964	Ken in Hawaii	1404	$125.00	
1964	Ken in Holland	0777	$145.00	
1964	Ken in Mexico	0778	$170.00	
1964	Ken in Switzerland	0776	$175.00	
1964	Ken Skin Diver	1406	$45.00	
1964	King Arthur	0773	$200.00	
1964	Lounging Around	Pak	N/A	
1964	Morning Workout	Pak	N/A	
1964	Party Fun	Pak	N/A	
1964	Prince, The	0772	$260.00	
1964	Roller Skate Date	1405	$75.00	
1964	Shoes for Sport	Pak	N/A	
1964	Skin Diver	3772	N/A	Sears
1964	Sleeper Set (blue)	0781	$60.00	
1964	Soda Date	Pak	N/A	
1964	Special Date	1401	$160.00	
1964	Sportsman	Pak	N/A	
1964	Top It Off	Pak	N/A	
1964	Victory Dance	1411	$155.00	
1964	White Is Right	Pak	N/A	
1964	Yatchsman, The (with cap)	789	$130.00	
1965	College Student	1416	$400.00	
1965	Here Comes the Groom	1426	$800.00	
1965	Hiking Holiday	1412	$185.00	
1965	Holiday	1414	$155.00	
1965	Mr. Astronaut	1415	$725.00	

KEN® OUTFITS

Listed by Year

YEAR	ITEM	NUMBER	VALUE	SPECIALS
1965	Off to Bed	1413	$130.00	
1965	Roller Skate Date (cap omitted, slacks added)	1405	$70.00	
1965	Rovin' Reporter	1417	$250.00	
1966	Business Appointment	1424	$975.00	
1966	Jazz Concert	1420	N/A	
1966	Ken A Go Go	1423	$450.00	
1966	Mountain Hike	1427	$180.00	
1966	Seein' the Sights	1421	$240.00	
1966	Summer Job	1422	$160.00	
1966	Time to Turn In	1418	$90.00	
1966	TV's Good Tonight	1419	$140.00	
1967	Pilot Uniform	1427	N/A	
1969	Breakfast at 7	1428	$40.00	
1969	Fabulous Formal Set	1595	N/A	
1969	Guruvy Formal	1431	$50.00	
1969	Rally Gear	1429	$65.00	
1969	Town Turtle	1430	$40.00	
1970	Bold Gold	1436	$40.00	
1970	Casual All-Stars	1436	N/A	
1970	Golf Gear	N/A	N/A	
1970	Shoe Ins	N/A	N/A	
1970	Slacks Are Back	N/A	N/A	
1970	Sun Fun	N/A	N/A	
1971	Casual Scene	1472	$40.00	
1971	Night Scene	1496	$65.00	
1971	Sea Scene	1449	$45.00	
1971	Skiing Scene	1438	$75.00	Get-Ups 'n Go
1971	Suede Scene	1439	$55.00	
1971	Surf's Up	1248	N/A	
1971	V.I.P. Scene	1473	$50.00	
1972	Beach Beat	3384	N/A	
1972	Brown on Brown	1718	$70.00	
1972	Casual Cords	1717	$60.00	
1972	Cook 'n Casual	3377	N/A	
1972	Denims for Fun	N/A	N/A	
1972	Midnight Blues	1719	$120.00	
1972	Mod Madras	1828	$90.00	
1972	Red, White, and Wild	1829	$30.00	
1972	Way-Out West	1720	$30.00	
1972	Western Winner	3377	N/A	

Christian Dior Barbie. The outfit is an adaptation of a Fall/Winter 1993–94 Haute Couture original by Gianfranco Ferré for Christian Dior. Limited edition of 50,000. Released fourth quarter of 1995.

FRANCIE® OUTFITS

Listed Alphabetically

ITEM	YEAR	NUMBER	VALUE
Although Elegant	1970	1242	$125.00
Although Elegant (reissue)	1974	1242	$60.00
Beach Outfit	1973	7710	N/A
Bells	1967	1275	$65.00
Bloom Zoom	1970	1239	$55.00
Bloom Zoom (reissue)	1974	1239	$35.00
Border-Line	1967	1287	$100.00
Bridal Beauty	1972	3288	N/A
Bridge Bit, The	1967	1279	$150.00
Brown Coat and Hat	1973	8646	N/A
Brown Skirt, Plaid Blouse	1973	8647	N/A
Buckeroo Blues	1971	3449	N/A
Camping	1974	7846	N/A
Candystriper	1973	7709	N/A
Casey Goes Casual Set	1967	Pak	N/A
Change-Offs	1971	3460	N/A
Check This	1967	1291	$110.00
Checker Chums	1972	3287	N/A
Checkmates	1966	1259	$110.00
Cheerleading Outfit	1973	7711	N/A
Clam Diggers	1966	1258	$125.0
Clear Out!	1967	1281	$275.00
Combination, The	1969	1234	$135.00
Combo, The	1968	1215	$140.00
Concert in the Park	1966	1256	$150.00
Cool Coveralls	1972	3281	N/A
Cool White	1967	1280	$170.00
Cool-It	1968	Pak	N/A
Corduroy Cape	1970	1764	N/A
Culotte-Wot?	1968	1214	$150.00
Dance Party	1966	1257	$185.00
Denims On!	1967	1290	$65.00
Double Ups	1972	3286	N/A
Dreamy Duo	1971	3450	N/A
Dreamy Duo (reissue)	1974	3450	N/A
Dreamy Wedding	1968	1217	$240.00
Entertainer, The	1970	1763	N/A
First Formal	1966	1260	$190.00
First Things First	1966	1252	$75.00
Floating-In	1968	1207	$225.00

FRANCIE® OUTFITS

Listed Alphabetically

Item	Year	Number	Value
Foot-Notes	1967	Pak	N/A
Foot-Notes	1968	Pak	N/A
For Francie Dressmakers	1967	Pak	N/A
Fresh as a Daisy	1966	1254	$130.00
Frosty Fur	1971	3455	N/A
Frosty Fur (reissue)	1974	3455	N/A
Fur Out	1966	1269	$450.00
Furry-Go-Round	1967	1294	$550.00
Gad-About	1966	1250	$130.00
Go Gold	1967	1294	$300.00
Gold Rush	1969	1222	$80.00
Groovy Get-Ups	1967	1270	N/A
Hair Dos	1968	Pak	N/A
Hair-Dos	1967	Pak	N/A
Hi-Teen	1967	1272	$60.00
Hill-Riders	1968	1210	$85.00
Hip Knits	1966	1265	$150.00
Ice Skating	1974	7485	N/A
Iced Blue	1967	1274	$75.00
In Step	1970	N/A	N/A
In-Print	1967	1288	$125.00
It's A Date	1966	1251	$85.00
Lace-Pace, The	1968	1216	$175.00
Land Ho!	1969	1220	$75.00
Lavender Dress	1974	7765	N/A
Lavender Jumper	1974	7764	N/A
Leather Limelight	1966	1269	$185.00
Little Knits	1972	3275	N/A
Long Dark Print Dress	1974	7769	N/A
Long on Leather	1970	1769	N/A
Long on Looks	1969	1227	$180.00
Long Red, White, Blue Halter Dress	1973	8644	N/A
Long White and Black Pin Dot	1974	7767	N/A
Long-View, The	1972	3282	N/A
Merry-Go-Rounders	1969	1230	$160.00
Midi Bouquet	1971	3446	N/A
Midi Duet	1971	3451	N/A
Midi Duet (reissue)	1974	3451	N/A
Midi Plaid	1971	3444	N/A
Mini-Chex	1968	1209	$65.00

Francie® Outfits

Listed Alphabetically

ITEM	YEAR	NUMBER	VALUE
Totally Terrific	1972	3280	N/A
Tuckered Out	1966	1253	$40.00
Tweed-Somes	1967	1286	$150.00
Twiggy Gear	1968	1728	N/A
Twiggy Turnouts	1968	1726	$180.00
Twiggy-Dos	1968	1725	$200.00
Twigster	1968	1727	$175.0
Twilight Twinkle	1971	3459	N/A
Two for the Ball	1969	1232	$150.00
Undies	1967	Pak	N/A
Vested Interest	1969	1224	$65.00
Victorian Wedding	1969	1233	$220.00
Waltz in Velvet	1970	1768	N/A
Wedding Whirl	1970	1244	$120.00
Wedding Whirl (reissue)	1974	1244	N/A
Western Wild	1970	N/A	N/A
Wild Bunch	1970	1766	N/A
Wild Flowers	1971	3456	N/A
Wild Flowers (reissue)	1974	3456	N/A
Wild 'n Wooly	1968	1218	$90.00
With-it-Whites	1971	3448	N/A
Yello Bit, The	1969	1223	$75.00
Zig-Zag Zoom	1971	3445	

FRANCIE® OUTFITS

Listed by Stock Number

NUMBER	ITEM	YEAR	VALUE
8649	Red Plaid Pants and Yellow and Blue Top	1973	N/A
9645	Short Red Print Dress	1973	N/A

The Barbie as Scarlett dolls, shown on these two pages, are the first in the Hollywood Legends Collection. There are four Barbie dolls and one Ken doll. The first Barbie as Scarlett doll wears the green drapery dress. She was followed by Ken as Rhett Butler, Barbie in the red velvet dress, barbecue dress, and honeymoon in New Orleans dress. The first doll was available in 1994, and the remaining came out in 1995. These dolls duplicate the gowns and hairstyles worn by Vivian Leigh in *Gone With the Wind*.

BOOKS & MAGAZINES

ITEM	YEAR	NUMBER	VALUE	SPECIALS
Mattel 1985 Answer Book	1985	N/A	$10.00	Mattel Toy Company
Mattel 1985 Catalog	1985	N/A	$8.00	Mattel Toy Company
Mattel 1986 Catalog	1986	N/A	$8.00	Mattel Toy Company
Mattel 1987 Catalog	1987	3692	$8.00	Mattel Toy Company
Mattel 1989 Catalog	1989	0313	$8.00	Mattel Toy Company
Mattel 1990 Catalog	1990	0470	$8.00	Mattel Toy Company
Mattel 1991 Catalog	1991	N/A	$20.00	Mattel Toy Company
Mattel 1995 Catalog for Girls	1995	13951	$5.00	Mattel Toy Company
Mini Posters	1974	N/A	$5.00	
Paint with Water	1993	1785-5	$2.00	Golden Books
Paint with Water	1993	1785-5	$2.00	Golden Books
Permanent Counter Catalog	1964	1084	N/A	
P.J. and Her Friends Sticker Fun	1972	N/A	$20.00	
Press-Out Book	N/A	N/A	N/A	
Scrap Book	1964	N/A	$50.00	
Sears Barbie Catalog Fall 1995	1995	N/A	$3.00	Sears
Sears Barbie Catalog Spring 1995	1995	N/A	$3.00	Sears
Skipper, Scott, and Beauty Sticker Fun Book	1980	N/A	$5.00	
Skipper, Skooter, Ricky	1965	N/A	$10.00	
Smithsonian, December 1989	1989	N/A	$25.00	
Sticker Album	1983	N/A	$10.00	
Sticker Fun Book	1991	N/A	$2.00	
Sticker Fun Book	1993	N/A	$2.00	
Sticker Fun Book	1994	8458	$2.00	
Story Diary	N/A	N/A	$5.00	
Sun Valley Barbie and Ken Sticker Fun	1975	N/A	$8.00	
Target's 30th Anniversary Barbie Keepsake	N/A	N/A	$15.00	Target
The Baby Sitter	1964	N/A	$5.00	Wonder Book
The Big Splash	1992	107-94	$2.00	Golden Books
The Fairy Princess (Superstar Barbie)	1977	111-38	$5.00	Golden Books
The Missing Wedding Dress	1986	107-63	$3.00	Golden Book
The World of Barbie	1963	533	N/A	Random House
The World of Barbie Fashion Book 1	1966	N/A	$5.00	
The World of Barbie Fashion Book 2	1967	N/A	$3.00	
The World Of Barbie Fashion Book 3	1966	N/A	$3.00	
The World of Barbie Magazine	1964	9904	N/A	
Trace and Color	1984	N/A	$3.00	
Western Barbie Coloring Book	1982	1146-2	$6.00	Golden Books

CASES

ITEM	YEAR	NUMBER	VALUE	STORE
4-Doll Trunk (Wedding Party)	1965	N/A	N/A	
Ballet Box	1969	5023	N/A	
Barbie & Francie Case	N/A	3003	N/A	
Barbie & Francie Dressing Room Case	1967	1024	N/A	
Barbie & Francie Hatbox	N/A	5020	N/A	
Barbie & Francie Overnighter	N/A	5022	N/A	
Barbie & Francie Train Case	N/A	5021	N/A	
Barbie & Ken Costume Trunk	N/A	5070	$100.00	
Barbie & Ken Trunk (orange blossom)	1964	N/A	N/A	
Barbie & Ken Trunk (tuxedo)	1964	N/A	N/A	
Barbie & Midge Case (blue)	1963	0204	N/A	J.C. Penney
Barbie & Midge Case (Lunch Date)	1963	N/A	$20.00	
Barbie & Midge Trunk (red)	1964	9330	N/A	Sears
Barbie or Midge Carry Case (black)	1963	4418	$20.00	Montgomery Ward
Barbie & Skipper Case	1965	N/A	N/A	
Barbie & Skipper Closet Carrier Playcase	1988	7222	N/A	
Barbie-Midge Case (pink) 18x4x14	1963	9330	N/A	Sears
Beach Party Case	1979	N/A	$100.00	Department Store
Black 4-Doll Case	1961	N/A	$15.00	
Blue Barbie Case	1962	N/A	$12.00	
Blue Trousseau Trunk	N/A	N/A	$100.00	
Carry-All	1972	4297	N/A	
Case	N/A	390	N/A	
Case, beige	N/A	N/A	$8.00	
Case (Easter Parade)	1961	N/A	$15.00	
Case (Enchanted Evening)	1963	N/A	$15.00	
Case (Red Flair)	1964	N/A	N/A	
Case with Doll	N/A	2000	N/A	
Double Doll Case	1989	2070	N/A	
Double Doll Sleep 'n Keep Case	1968	N/A	N/A	
Double Fashion Doll Case	1986	2811	N/A	
Fashion Doll Trunk	1980	1004	N/A	
Fashion Queen Barbie Carrying Case	N/A	N/A	$75.00	
Francie Case	N/A	1023	N/A	
Francie Case	N/A	3002	N/A	
Francie & Casey Case	N/A	1027	N/A	
Francie & Casey Double Case	N/A	1025	N/A	
Goes Travelin' Blue Carrying Case	N/A	N/A	$75.00	
Goes Travelin' Pink Carrying Case	N/A	N/A	$75.00	
Goes Travelin' Yellow Carrying Case	N/A	N/A	$75.00	

CASES

ITEM	YEAR	NUMBER	VALUE	STORE
Green and White Diamond Case	1964	479	$1800.00	
Hat Box	1962	4402	N/A	Montgomery Ward
House Mate Case	1965	N/A	$50.00	
Jamie's Room Case	1971	31121	N/A	Sears
Ken and Allen Case (France)	N/A	Foreign	$300.00	
Ken Case, Aqua, 11x4x13	1963	9328	$12.00	Sears
Ken Case (Campus Hero)	1964	N/A	N/A	
Ken Case (Rally Day)	1963	N/A	N/A	
Large Barbie Doll Case	1962	N/A	$15.00	
Lavender Ken Case	1961	N/A	$15.00	
Loving Care Play Case	1988	4927	N/A	
Midge Case (Movie Date)	1964	N/A	N/A	
Midge Case (red)	1964	9381	N/A	Sears
Miss Barbie Black Patent Leather	1963	N/A	$165.00	
Miss Barbie Carrying Case	N/A	Case	$75.00	
My First Barbie Dance and Dress Case	1989	2071	N/A	
One Doll Room Case	1971	N/A	N/A	Sears
Overnight Case	N/A	4295	N/A	
Overnite Case	1972	4295	N/A	
Plane-Car Case	1965	N/A	N/A	
Pony Tail Case	1962	N/A	$65.00	
Red Barbie and Midge Case	N/A	N/A	$150.00	Europe
Silver Screen Barbie	1994	N/A	$45.00	F.A.O. Schwarz
Single Doll Case	1981	1002	N/A	Golden Dream
Single Doll Case	1986	2810	N/A	
Single Doll Case	1989	2069	N/A	
Skipper Case	N/A	360	N/A	
Skipper Case	19	1045	N/A	
Skipper Case	1970	4966	N/A	
Skipper Case (School Days)	1964	N/A	N/A	
Skipper Case with Doll	N/A	2001	N/A	
Skipper & Skooter Case	1965	N/A	N/A	
Skooter Case with Doll	N/A	2002	N/A	
Sleep 'n Keep Case	1969	30471	N/A	Sears
Stacie Case	N/A	1046	N/A	
Tote Bag	1972	4296	N/A	
Travel Case	1961	N/A	$20.00	
Travel Case #2	1961	N/A	$20.00	
Travel Trunk	N/A	4289	N/A	
Travel Vanity Case Barbie & Skipper	1965	N/A	N/A	

CASES

ITEM	YEAR	NUMBER	VALUE	STORE
Trunk Carries All #3, 10x7x13	1963	9331	N/A	Sears
Trunk (Solo in the Spotlight)	1963	N/A	N/A	
Tutti and Chris Patio Picnic Case	N/A	N/A	$35.00	
Tutti Case	N/A	3023	N/A	
Tutti Case	N/A	3561	N/A	
Tutti Hatbox	N/A	5016	N/A	
Tutti Overnighter	N/A	5018	N/A	
Tutti Play Case	N/A	3001	N/A	
Tutti Train Case	N/A	5017	N/A	
Two Doll Sleep 'n Keep Case	1968	N/A	N/A	Sears
Two Doll Trunk	1981	1004	N/A	Golden Dream
Two Doll Trunk	1984	1004	N/A	
White 4-Doll Case	1961	N/A	$8.00	
White, Tutti Wears Swing A Ling	N/A	N/A	$45.00	
White with Francie in Mod Clothes	N/A	N/A	$95.00	
World of Barbie, 2-Doll Trunk	1969	1004	N/A	
World of Barbie Doll Case	1969	1007	N/A	
World of Barbie Single Doll Case	1969	1002	N/A	

Children's Clothes

Item	Year	Number	Value	Store
Blouse, Multicolor (sizes 7 – 12)	1964	4388F	N/A	Sears
Bra, Panty, and Pettipant	1963	5320	N/A	
Chelsen Blouse (sizes 7 – 14)	1964	4386F	N/A	Sears
Girls Tennis Shoes, sizes 10 – 2	1995	N/A	$12.00	Pay Less Shoe Store
Jacket (blue and white, sizes 7 – 14)	1964	4396F	N/A	Sears
Jacket (bright rose and white, sizes 7 – 14)	1964	4397F	N/A	Sears
Jumper (blue and white, sizes 7 – 14)	1964	4395F	N/A	Sears
Jumper (bright rose and white, sizes 7 – 14)	1964	4394F	N/A	Sears
Mix and Match Separates	1962	1754	N/A	Montgomery Ward
Peignoir and Sleeveless Pajama Set	1963	5319	N/A	
Skirt #2 (blue and white, sizes 7 – 14)	1964	4392F	N/A	Sears
Skirt #2 (bright rose and white, sizes 7 – 14)	1964	74393F	N/A	Sears
Skirt (blue and white, sizes 7 – 14)	1964	4391F	N/A	Sears
Skirt (bright rose and white, sizes 7 – 14)	1964	4390F	N/A	Sears

ENESCO

ITEM	YEAR	NUMBER	VALUE	SPECIAL
After Five Figurine	1994	353647	$25.00	Fashion Barbie Series
Ballerina 1961	1994	113875	$5.00	Classic Barbie Figurine
Bride's Dream Musical	1995	113905	$100.00	Glamour Collection Series
Brochures	1994	BAR005	$12.00	Fashion Barbie Series
Buttons	1995	BAR001	$15.00	From Barbie with Love
Career Girl 1963 Ceramic Mug	1994	124435	$14.00	From Barbie with Love
Display Mini Figure	1994	BAR010	$120.00	Classic Barbie
Display with 50 Brochures	1994	BAR004	$20.00	Fashion Barbie Series
Enchanted Evening 1960 Porcelain Bust	1995	115266	$70.00	From Barbie with Love
Enchanted Evening 1960	1994	133396	$5.00	Classic Barbie Figurine
Enchanted Evening 1960 Ceramic Mug	1994	124443	$14.00	From Barbie with Love
Enchanted Evening 1960 Musical	1994	353620	$100.00	From Barbie with Love
Evening Splendor 1959 Miniature Bust	1995	125601	$2.00	From Barbie with Love
Gay Parisienne 1959 Miniature Bust	1995	125601	$2.00	From Barbie with Love
Graduation 1963 Vase	1994	124419	$15.00	From Barbie with Love
Graduation Mini Figure	1994	113867	$5.00	Classic Barbie
Let's Go To The Hop (Music Box)	1994	551538	$120.00	From Barbie with Love
Midnight Blue 1965 Musical	1995	113891	$100.00	Glamour Collection Series
Original Swimsuit 1959 Figurine	1995	113700	$30.00	Fashion Collection Series
Picnic 1959 Figurine	1995	113727	$30.00	Fashion Collection Series
Plantation Belle 1959 Miniature Bust	1995	125601	$2.00	From Barbie with Love
Poodle Parade 1965 Figurine	1995	113719	$30.00	Fashion Collection Series
Red Flare	1994	353701	$25.00	Fashion Barbie Series
Registered Nurse 1961 Ceramic Mug	1994	124427	$14.00	From Barbie with Love
Registered Nurse 1961 Vase	1994	124397	$15.00	From Barbie with Love
Salt Pepper Shaker (Ken & Barbie)	1995	113921	$15.00	From Barbie with Love
Senior Prom 1963 Musical	1995	124370	$100.00	From Barbie with Love
Senior Prom 1963 Musical	1995	125776	$100.00	Glamour Collection Series
Senior Prom 1963 Vase	1994	124400	$15.00	From Barbie with Love
Solo in the Spotlight 1960 Musical	1994	353752	$100.00	From Barbie with Love
Solo in the Spotlight 1960 Vase	1994	124389	$15.00	From Barbie with Love
Solo in the Spotlight Plate	1995	114383	$30.00	From Barbie with Love
Sophisticated Lady Musical	1995	113883	$100.00	Glamour Collection Series
Suburban Shopper 1959 Figurine	1995	113751	$30.00	Fashion Collection Series
Wedding Day 1959	1994	113859	$5.00	Classic Barbie Figurine
Wedding Day 1959 Miniature Bust	1995	125601	$2.00	From Barbie with Love
Wedding Day 1959 Musical	1994	333639	$100.00	From Barbie with Love

GIFT SETS

ITEM	YEAR	NUMBER	VALUE	STORE
Trousseau Set	1960	858	$2100.00	
Twirly Curls Gift Set	1983	N/A	N/A	Department Store
Twist 'n Turn P.J. Gift Set	1970	30816	N/A	Sears
Vacation Sensation Gift Set	1983	N/A	N/A	Toys 'R' Us
Vacation Sensation Gift Set (pink)	1987	N/A	N/A	Toys 'R' Us
Walking Jamie Furry Friends Set	1970	1584	$300.00	Sears
Walking Jamie Strollin' In Style	1972	1247	$425.00	Sears
Walking Jamie with Dog Gift Set	1970	30813	$250.00	Sears
Wedding Fantasy Gift Set	1993	N/A	$95.00	Wholesale Clubs
Wedding Party Deluxe Set	1994	13557	$30.00	Toys 'R' Us
Wedding Party Gift Set	1964	1017	$2000.00	
Western Stampin' Gift Set	1993	11020	$30.00	Wholesale Clubs

Dutch Barbie, issued in 1994, is part of the Dolls of the World Collection. She wears shoes that are shaped like Dutch wooden shoes.

Abbe Littleton, a Mattel designer for many years, designed Midnight Gala Barbie doll. Her make-up is beautiful. Her black velvet cape and gown are covered in holographic glitter, which sparkles in rainbow colors and matches the sequins on her bodice, earrings, and hairpiece. She is the fourth doll in the Classique series. She was offered in 1995, and a tag inside her gown bears the designer's name.

"We girls can do anything" is the Barbie doll's slogan on her Career Collection boxes. Toys 'R' Us has an endless array of store special Barbie dolls. Pictured here are two from the Career Collection series. The police officer was offered in 1994 and the firefighter was offered in 1995.

In 1993 Barbie and Ken dolls served in the army during Desert Storm. These dolls were sold separately and together. They are also available in a black version. They are part of the Stars 'n Stripes series.

Jewelry

Item	Year	Number	Value	Store/Collection
16th Anniversary Child's Pendant	1974	N/A	$12.00	
35th Anniversary Watch	1994	N/A	$150.00	Fossil Watches
Barbie and Me Jewels and Chest	1963	1771	N/A	
Barbie for Girls Neon Orange Watch	1992	N/A	$10.00	
Bracelet for You	1988	4632	N/A	Perfume Pretty Jewelry
Cameo Bracelet	1982	5114	N/A	
Cameo Locket	1982	5115	N/A	
Cameo Ring	1982	5116	N/A	
Charm Bracelet Watch	1994	N/A	$200.00	Fossil Watches
Costume Jewelry Set	1962	1311	N/A	Sears
Diamond Collection	1987	1928	N/A	
Electric Wristwatch Wall Clock	N/A	N/A	$40.00	
Ermerald Collection	1987	1924	N/A	
Fan Club Bracelet	N/A	N/A	$15.00	
Fan Club Promotional Wristwatch	1981	N/A	$40.00	
Fashion Coordinated Jewelry	1962	1759	N/A	Montgomery Ward
Gold Collection	1987	1923	$5.00	
Gold Medal Jewelry	1975	8059	$15.00	
Jewel Secrets Collector Case	1987	3763	N/A	
Jewelry and Purse for Barbie	1988	4637	N/A	Perfume Pretty Jewelry
Jewelry, Belt, Shoes for Barbie	1988	4635	N/A	Perfume Pretty Jewelry
Jewelry Gift Set	1982	5247	N/A	
Jewelry, Hair Comb, and Belt	1988	4633	N/A	Perfume Pretty Jewelry
Name Tags	N/A	N/A	$2.00	
Necklace Bronze Color	N/A	N/A	$15.00	
Nostalgic Pin	1989	N/A	$20.00	
Offical Wristwatch	1980	N/A	$50.00	
Pendant for You	1988	4634	N/A	Perfume Pretty Jewelry
Perfume Pretty Gifts for Two	1988	5558	N/A	Perfume Pretty Jewelry
Pink Watch	N/A	N/A	$50.00	
Play Jewelry	N/A	N/A	$152.00	
Play Ring	N/A	N/A	$100.00	
Ponytail Wristwatches #1	N/A	N/A	N/A	
Ponytail Wristwatches #2	N/A	N/A	N/A	
Ponytail Wristwatches #3	N/A	N/A	N/A	
Pretty in Pink Watch	1994	N/A	$125.00	Fossil Watches
Red Jewelry Box	1963	N/A	$25.00	
Ring for You	1988	4635	N/A	Perfume Pretty Jewelry
Ruby Collection	1987	1929	N/A	
Sapphire Collection	1987	1927	N/A	

JEWELRY

ITEM	YEAR	NUMBER	VALUE	STORE/COLLECTION
Silver Collection	1987	1926	N/A	
Silver Screen Watch	1994	N/A	$125.00	Fossil Watches
Single Charm Bracelet	1963	N/A	$75.00	
Starbright Boudoir Clock	N/A	N/A	$50.00	
Style Magic Hair Charms & Barrettes	1989	1649	N/A	
Sweet 16 Promotional Necklace	N/A	7796	$100.00	
Swirl Watch (blue band)	N/A	N/A	$85.00	
Swirl Watch (yellow band)	N/A	N/A	$95.00	
Three-piece Jewelry Set	1963	N/A	$45.00	
Twist 'n Turn Watch Blue Rim	1971	N/A	$125.00	
Watch (necklace type)	1964	N/A	N/A	
Watch Promotional Fan Club	1981	N/A	$50.00	
Watch with ¾ face looking left	1963	N/A	$50.00	
Wristwatch (blue dial and band)	1964	N/A	N/A	J.C. Penney
Wristwatch (red dial and band)	1964	N/A	N/A	
Wristwatch with 3 changeable bands	1969	5211	$95.00	
Wristwatch with large dial	N/A	N/A	$50.00	
Wristwatch with small dial	N/A	N/A	$50.00	

MAKE-UP

ITEM	YEAR	NUMBER	VALUE	STORE/COLLECTION
3-piece Dresser Set	1962	1383	N/A	Sears
Beauty Bath Set for Two	1988	5560	N/A	Perfume Pretty Bath
Beauty Kit	1961	N/A	$100.00	
Beauty Parlor Set	1963	8643	N/A	
Beauty Sets	1982	5119	N/A	Just for You
Blush, peach	1982	5131	N/A	Just for You
Blush, pink	1981	3591	N/A	Just for You
Blush, plum	1982	5132	N/A	Just for You
Blush, red	1981	3593	N/A	Just for You
Body Lotion and Bow Barrette for 2	1988	5537	N/A	Perfume Pretty Bath
Cameo Barrette, blue	1982	5216	N/A	Just for You
Cameo Barrette, lilac	1982	5222	N/A	Just for You
Cameo Barrette, pink	1982	5090	N/A	Just for You
Cameo Barrette, yellow	1982	5219	N/A	Just for You
Cameo Case	1982	3894	N/A	Just for You
Cameo Comb, blue	1982	5217	N/A	Just for You
Cameo Comb, lilac	1982	5223	N/A	Just for You
Cameo Comb, pink	1982	5091	N/A	Just for You
Cameo Comb, yellow	1982	5220	N/A	Just for You
Cameo Ponytail Holder, blue	1982	5218	N/A	Just for You
Cameo Ponytail Holder, lilac	1982	5224	N/A	Just for You
Cameo Ponytail Holder, pink	1982	5089	N/A	Just for You
Cameo Ponytail Holder, yellow	1982	5221	N/A	Just for You
Cologne	1961	N/A	$125.00	
Cologne	1981	3603	N/A	Just for You
Cosmetics Case	1981	3548	N/A	Just for You
Dusting Powder and Powder Mitt for 2	1988	5552	N/A	Perfume Pretty Bath
Eye Shadow lemon/orchard/pink	1982	5133	N/A	Just for You
Eye Shadow, lilac/sea blue/rose	1981	3609	N/A	Just for you
Eye Shadow power blue/aqua/warm brown	1981	3596	N/A	Just for You
Eye Shadow, sky blue/peach/plum	1981	3595	N/A	Just for You
Fragrance and Perfume Purse for 2	1988	5536	N/A	Perfume Pretty Bath
Glamour Cosmetics	1963	8643	N/A	
Hair Beauty Set, light blue	1982	5214	N/A	Just for You
Hair Beauty Set, pink	1982	5215	N/A	Just for You
I'm into Barbie Hair Brush and Comb	1989	N/A	$10.00	Avon
Lip Gloss and Mirror for 2	1988	5554	N/A	Perfume Pretty Bath
Lip Gloss, apple	1982	5175	N/A	Just for You
Lip Gloss, cherry	1982	5172	N/A	Just for You
Lip Gloss, plum	1982	5174	N/A	Just for You

Make-up

Item	Year	Number	Value	Store/Collection
Lip Gloss, watermelon	1982	5173	N/A	Just for You
Lipstick, coral (tropical fruit)	1981	3589	N/A	Just for You
Lipstick, grape	1982	5135	N/A	Just for You
Lipstick, hot pink (bubblegum)	1981	3590	N/A	Just for You
Lipstick, pastel pink (peppermint)	1981	3587	N/A	Just for You
Lipstick, red (strawberry)	1981	3588	N/A	Just for You
Lipstick, tangerine	1982	5134	N/A	Just for You
Liquid Soap and Sponge for 2	1988	5551	N/A	Perfume Pretty Bath
Lotion	1961	N/A	$125.00	
Make-Up Case	1963	N/A	$25.00	
Nail Polish, coral	1981	3585	N/A	Just for You
Nail Polish, deep violet	1982	5130	N/A	Just for You
Nail Polish, hot pink	1981	3586	N/A	Just for You
Nail Polish, pastel pink	1981	3583	N/A	Just for You
Nail Polish, red	1981	3584	N/A	Just for You
Perfume Maker Set	1980	2740	N/A	
Pink Shades Beauty Set	1981	3598	N/A	Just for You
Red Shades Beauty Set	1981	3599	N/A	Just for You
Shampoo and Comb for 2	1988	5557	N/A	Perfume Pretty Bath

MISCELLANEOUS

ITEM	YEAR	NUMBER	VALUE	STORE/COLLECTION
1st Edition Trading Club	1990	N/A	$50.00	
8 Broad Line Markers	1994	8760	$6.00	
8 Fine Line Markers	1994	8757	$2.00	
8-in-One Costume	1962	840F	N/A	Sears
8-piece Set (McDonalds)	1991	N/A	$30.00	McDonalds
8-piece Set (McDonalds)	1992	N/A	$30.00	McDonalds
8-piece Set (McDonalds)	1994	N/A	$28.00	McDonalds
12 Brilliant Colored Pencils	1994	9465	$3.00	
16 Crayons	1994	5593	$3.00	
24 Crayons	1994	5344	$6.00	
25th Anniversay Tea Set	1984	N/A	$75.00	
30th Anniversary Calendar	1989	N/A	$20.00	
30th Anniversary Commemorative Coin	1989	N/A	$25.00	
35th Anniversary Tea Set	1994	N/A	$40.00	Chilto Toys
1991 Calender	1991	241	$10.00	
AM Radio Shape of Barbie	1980	5203	$10.00	
AM-FM Radio System	1984	20041	$15.00	Power Tronics
Ballerina Barbie Dress-Up Kit	1977	616	$10.00	
Barbie and Beauty Fashion Dress-Up Kit	1981	2363	$5.00	
Barbie and Ken Talking Alarm Clock	1983	8120	$15.00	
Barbie and Me Vanity Set	1962	4719	N/A	Montgomery Ward
Barbie and Midge Black Thermos	1965	N/A	$25.00	
Barbie and Midge Domed Lunch Box	1965	N/A	$250.00	
Barbie and Midge Lunch Box	1963	N/A	$50.00	
Barbie and Midge Thermos Bottles	1963	N/A	$20.00	
Barbie and Stacey Fashion Boutique	N/A	N/A	$1000.00	Store Display
Barbie Doll Fashion Patterns	1962	837	N/A	
Barbie Doll Fashion Patterns #2	1963	837	N/A	
Barbie Fashion Embroidery Set	1964	7502A	N/A	
Barbie, Ken, Midge Embroidery Set	1963	7686	N/A	
Barbie & Me Dress-Up Set	N/A	N/A	$75.00	
Barbie & Skipper Electric Drawing Set	N/A	N/A	$25.00	
Beauty Secrets	N/A	N/A	$300.00	Store Display
Best Buys Fashion Offer (shelf strip)	1982	5352	N/A	Store Display
Book Bag	1984	7483	N/A	On the Go
Breakfast with Barbie Cereal	1989	16609	$10.00	
Calendar by Gibson	1992	N/A	$10.00	
Campus Queen Lunch Box and Thermos	1967	N/A	$20.00	
Canvas Tote Bags	N/A	N/A	$30.00	
Cassette Player	1981	3742	N/A	

MISCELLANEOUS

Item	Year	Number	Value	Store/Collection
Christmas Stockings	N/A	N/A	$30.00	Joey Skilbred
Cleaning Set	1982	569	$10.00	
Clear Jelly Clogs, Girls Sizes	1993	N/A	$10.00	Payless Shoe Store
Colorforms Barbie Dressup Set Travel Pak	1989	361	$2.00	
Cutlery Set	1962	941	N/A	Sears
Danbury Mint Collector Plates, set of 8	N/A	N/A	$300.00	
Desk Calculator	1981	3457	N/A	
Dr. Ken Kit	1963	1959	N/A	
Dream House Play Set	1979	N/A	$12.00	
Electric Drawing Set	1963	1985	N/A	Sears
Evening Outfit for Girls	1963	1772	N/A	
Fan on Board Window Suction	1990	N/A	$10.00	
Fashion Greeting Cards (all occasion)	1995	13041	N/A	
Fashion Greeting Cards (birthday)	1995	13024	N/A	
Fashion Greeting Cards (holiday)	1995	13062	N/A	
Fashion Maker Set	1981	3271	N/A	
Fluorescent Water Colors	1994	9451	$3.00	
FM Microphone	1981	3456	N/A	
Free Cologne Sampler (shelf strip)	1982	N/A	N/A	Store Display
Free Cosmetic Bag Offer (shelf strip)	1982	5351	N/A	Store Display
Friendship Collection	1981	9001	$10.00	
Fur and Jewels Safe	1978	2595	$10.00	
GAF Viewmaster Barbie Around the World	1965	N/A	$150.00	
Ge-Tar	1964	0524	N/A	
Gibson Ballerina Barbie Birthday Card	1989	N/A	$2.00	
Gift Wrap by Gibson	1988	N/A	$10.00	
Gift Wrap (nostalgic papers)	1994	N/A	$15.00	
Good Grooming Manicure Set	N/A	N/A	$75.00	
Hallmark Barbie Calendar	1995	N/A	$15.00	
Hallmark Christmas Ornament	1993	N/A	$75.00	
Hallmark Christmas Ornament	1994	05216	$45.00	
Hallmark Easter Ornament	1995	08069	$25.00	
Hallmark Glamour Dream Collection	1994	N/A	$25.00	
Hallmark Nostalgic in Swimsuit Ornament	1994	N/A	$45.00	
Halloween Costume	1973	N/A	$75.00	
Heirloom Set	1962	4635	N/A	Montgomery Ward
Hula Hoop	1991	N/A	$10.00	
Inflatable Pool 54"	1993	1652	$15.00	
Julia Dress-Up Kit	1969	N/A	$10.00	
Ken Wardrobe Patterns	1962	834	N/A	

MISCELLANEOUS

Item	Year	Number	Value	Store/Collection
Knitting for Barbie	1962	4767	N/A	Montgomery Ward
Knitting Kit	1962	N/A	$30.00	
Large Barbie Photo Album	1963	N/A	$50.00	
Luncheon Embroidery Set	1962	4648D	N/A	Montgomery Ward
Mattel Doll Pattern Assortment	1962	836	N/A	
Mattel-A-Phone	N/A	N/A	$100.00	
McCalls Pattern, Girls Nightgown	N/A	7545	$25.00	
Midge Fashion Embroidery Set	1964	7538A	N/A	
Miniature Nostalgic Tea Set	1994	N/A	$30.00	
Modern Miss Play Box	1963	593	N/A	Sears
Nostalgic Special 16 Month Edition Calendar	1990	N/A	$20.00	
Nurse Kit	1962	1694	N/A	Sears
Patterns	1961	4171	N/A	Advance
Pencil Set	1984	7488	N/A	On the Go
Pillow 18x8	N/A	N/A	$35.00	Joey Skilbred
Pillow Cases	1991	N/A	$5.00	
Plastic Dishes	1963	N/A	$20.00	
Purse, Shoe Sets	1964	3295	N/A	Sears
Queen of the Prom Costume with Wig	1962	817F	N/A	Sears
Radio	1981	3455	N/A	
Record Player (red)	1961	N/A	$200.00	Montgomery Ward
Record Tote	1961	N/A	$40.00	
Sew Magic Add Ons for Francie & Skipper	1973	N/A	$20.00	
Sewing Accessories	1964	3294	N/A	Sears
Shoulder Bag	1984	7481	N/A	On the Go
Skipper Blue Coin Purse	1964	N/A	$30.00	
Skipper Blue Wallet	1964	N/A	$30.00	
Snap Shot Album	1963	N/A	$40.00	
Sneak Preview Calendar	1991	N/A	$10.00	
Sports Fashion Set	1975	2352	$5.00	
Spring Canvas Wallet	N/A	N/A	$7.00	
Spring Green Canvas Wallet	N/A	N/A	$7.00	
Super Star Cameramatic Flash Camera	1978	8503	$20.00	
Sweet 16 Promotional Set	1974	7796	N/A	
Table Cloth	1978	N/A	$25.00	
Tea Set	1960	991	N/A	Sears
Tea Set (42-piece)	1962	942	N/A	Sears
Tea Set (44-piece)	1964	4842	N/A	J.C. Penney
Tea Set (44-piece)	1965	4702	N/A	Sears
Tea Set (46-piece)	1963	8689	N/A	

MISCELLANEOUS

ITEM	YEAR	NUMBER	VALUE	STORE/COLLECTION
Tea Set (56-piece)	1961	4759	N/A	Montgomery Ward
Tea Set (62-piece)	1962	4759	N/A	Montgomery Ward
Tea Set (62-piece)	1965	951	N/A	Sears
Thermos	1962	N/A	$40.00	
Toothbrush	1981	3458	N/A	
Towel & Wash Cloth	N/A	N/A	$15.00	
Umbrella for Girls	1962	N/A	$65.00	
Wallet	1984	7478	N/A	On the Go
Western Barbie Dress Up Set	1982	657	$5.00	
Western Barbie Dress-Up Set	1981	635	$15.00	
Wonderful World of Barbie, The	N/A	N/A	$900.00	Store Display
Workout Bag	1984	7480	N/A	On the Go
World of Barbie, The	1965	1093	$1000.00	Store Display

PAPER DOLLS

ITEM	YEAR	NUMBER	VALUE
2 Magic Dolls with Stay-On Clothes	1969	N/A	$35.00
Angel Face	1983	N/A	$7.00
Angel Face Barbie (boxed)	1983	N/A	$10.00
Ballerina Barbie (boxed)	1977	N/A	$6.00
Barbie and Francie Magic Stay-On Fashions	1966	N/A	N/A
Barbie and Ken	1984	1585-51	$10.00
Barbie and Ken All Sport Tournament	1976	N/A	$8.00
Barbie and Ken Cut Outs	1962	N/A	$25.00
Barbie and the Rockers	1986	N/A	$8.00
Barbie (boxed)	1983	N/A	$8.00
Barbie Doll	1990	1523-2	$6.00
Barbie & Her Friends	N/A	N/A	$6.00
Barbie & Ken	1962	N/A	N/A
Barbie & Ken	1970	N/A	N/A
Barbie & Ken Paper Doll	1974	N/A	$25.00
Barbie, Skipper, and Skooter Cut Out	1966	N/A	$20.00
Barbie & Skipper (with playbook)	N/A	N/A	$7.00
Beach Bus	N/A	N/A	$6.00
Christmas Barbie	1984	N/A	$12.00
Christmas Time	1984	N/A	$15.00
Cover Girl P.J.	1971	N/A	$25.00
Crystal Barbie	1984	N/A	$4.00
Crystal Barbie and Ken	1984	N/A	$5.00
Crystal Barbie (boxed)	1984	N/A	$7.00
Day to Night	1985	N/A	$8.00
Deluxe Paper Dolls	1991	1695	$3.00
Fantasy Barbie	N/A	N/A	$4.00
Fashion Originals	N/A	N/A	$10.00
Fashion Photo	1979	N/A	$12.00
Fashion Photo Barbie (boxed)	N/A	N/A	$15.00
Francie with Pretty Growin' Hair	1973	N/A	$50.00
Friendship Paper Dolls	1973	N/A	$15.00
Goin' Campin' with P.J.	1974	N/A	$15.00
Golden Dream	N/A	N/A	$6.00
Golden Dream Barbie (boxed)	N/A	N/A	$12.00
Great Shape Barbie	1985	N/A	N/A
Groovin' World of Barbie and Her Friends	1971	N/A	$15.00
Growing Up Skipper	N/A	N/A	$7.00
Jeans Barbie Poster Book	N/A	N/A	$3.00
Jewel Secrets	1987	N/A	$8.00

PAPER DOLLS

ITEM	YEAR	NUMBER	VALUE
Julia	1968	N/A	$50.00
Kissing Barbie (boxed)	N/A	N/A	$12.00
Live Action Barbie Magic Paper Doll	1971	N/A	$10.00
Malibu Barbie (boxed)	1982	N/A	$10.00
Malibu Francie	1973	N/A	$15.00
Malibu Francie	1976	N/A	$20.00
Malibu P.J. Magic Paper Dolls	1972	N/A	$5.00
Malibu Skipper	1973	1069	$10.00
Malibu Sunset Barbie	1972	N/A	$10.00
New and Groovy P.J. Paper Dolls	1970	N/A	$25.00
Paper Dolls	1962	N/A	$125.00
Paper Dolls	1992	N/A	$3.00
Peaches 'n Cream	N/A	N/A	N/A
Perfume Pretty	1988	N/A	$5.00
Pink & Pretty	N/A	1427	$7.00
Pink & Pretty Barbie (boxed)	1983	N/A	$10.00
Pink & Pretty (with playbook)	N/A	N/A	$10.00
Press Out	1985	N/A	$5.00
Pretty Changes	N/A	N/A	$8.00
Pretty Changes (boxed)	N/A	N/A	$15.00
Quick Curl Barbie	1975	N/A	$12.00
Quick Curl Barbie (boxed)	N/A	N/A	$15.00
Quick Curl Barbie, Francie, Kelley, Skipper	1973	N/A	$20.00
Skipper	1975	N/A	$12.00
Sunsational Barbie	1983	N/A	$3.00
Sunsational Barbie and Ken	1983	N/A	$5.00
Sunsational Malibu Barbie	1983	N/A	$5.00
Super Star Barbie	1978	N/A	$12.00
Super Star Barbie (boxed)	1989	N/A	$15.00
Super Teen Skipper	1980	N/A	$8.00
Super Teen Skipper & Scott (boxed)	1981	N/A	$15.00
Superstar	1989	N/A	$5.00
Sweet 16	1974	N/A	$12.00
TNT and Talker	1969	N/A	$20.00
Twirl Curls Barbie	N/A	N/A	$4.00
Western Barbie	1983	N/A	$6.00
Western Barbie (boxed)	1982	N/A	$10.00
Western Skipper (boxed)	1983	N/A	$10.00

PETS

ITEM	YEAR	NUMBER	VALUE
Animal Lovin' Animal Assortment	1989	3499	$25.00
Animal Lovin' Ginger Giraffe	1988	1395	$25.00
Animal Lovin' Zizi Zebra	1988	1393	$25.00
Beauty	1980	1018	N/A
Beauty and Puppies	1981	5019	$30.00
Blinking Beauty Horse	1988	5087	N/A
Dallas (horse)	1981	3312	N/A
Dancer (horse)	1971	1157	$50.00
Dream Horse Dixie	1984	7073	$29.00
Dream Horse Prancer	1984	7263	$29.00
Fluff	1983	5524	$55.00
Flying Hero Horse	1995	14265	$25.00
High Stepper Walking Horse	1995	11766	$25.00
Honey (pony)	1983	5880	N/A
Midnight (horse)	1982	5337	N/A
Mitzi Meow Cat	1994	11070	$10.00
Prancing Horse	1994	11766	$30.00
Prince (French poodle)	1985	7928	N/A
Puppy Ruff Dog	1994	11069	$10.00
Sachi, Barbie doll's Dog	1991	N/A	$18.00
Snowball Her Pet Dog	1990	N/A	$18.00
Spirit (horse)	1994	11550	$25.00
Sun Runner (horse)	1990	9961	$45.00
Tag-A-Long Tiffy	1992	3352	$10.00
Tag-A-Long Wags	1992	N/A	$15.00
Tropical Splash Seahorse	1995	12436	$10.00
Tropical Tahaiti (bird)	1965	2064	$25.00

REAL ESTATE

ITEM	YEAR	NUMBER	VALUE	STORE/COLLECTION
Action Beauty Scene	1971	1016	N/A	
Action Sewing Center	1972	4026	N/A	
All Stars Sports Club	1990	4972	N/A	
Apartment	1975	9188	$60.00	Department Store
Ballerina Barbie Stage	1976	9651	N/A	
Barbie & Francie Campus	1966	4093	N/A	
Barbie & Ken Little Theater	1964	4090	$300.00	
Barbie Loves McDonalds	1983	5559	N/A	
Barbie & Skipper Deluxe Dream Hosue	1965	9342L	N/A	Sears
Beach Blast Patio & Pool	1989	3593	N/A	
Beauty Salon	1983	4839	N/A	
Bedroom Accents	1986	2375	N/A	
Boutique	1971	31129	N/A	Sears
Bubble Gum and Gift Shop	1995	12710	N/A	
California Dream Surf 'n Shop	1988	4461	N/A	
Campus	1964	9303	N/A	Sears
Cookin' Fun Kitchen	1971	4987	N/A	Barbie's Place Setting
Cool Tops T-Shirt Shop	1990	4955	N/A	
Country Living House	1973	8662	$75.00	
Deluxe Dream House	1966	N/A	N/A	
Dream Cottage (furnished)	1983	4718	N/A	
Dream Cottage (unfurnished)	1983	4432	N/A	
Dream House	1962	816	N/A	
Dream House	1964	4092	N/A	
Dream House (furnished)	1980	2587	N/A	
Dream House (furnished)	1988	1667	N/A	
Dream House (unfurnished)	1980	2588	N/A	
Dream Kitchen-Dinette	1965	4095	N/A	
Dream Pool (no furniture)	1981	1481	N/A	
Dream Pool (with furniture)	1981	1496	N/A	
Dream Room	1965	4094	$250.00	
Dream Store Deluxe Set	1983	4022	N/A	
Dream Store Makeup Department	1983	4020	N/A	
Family Deluxe House	1966	N/A	N/A	
Family House	1967	1055	$35.00	
Fashion Plaza	1976	9525	N/A	
Fashion Salon	1964	9306L	N/A	Sears
Fashion Shop	1962	817	$150.00	
Fashion Stage	1971	1148	$50.00	
Fashion Wraps Boutique	1989	4024	N/A	

REAL ESTATE

ITEM	YEAR	NUMBER	VALUE	STORE/COLLECTION
Fold 'n Fun House	1994	1545	$50.00	
Fountain Pool	1994	12650	$30.00	
Francie & Casey Studio House	1967	1026	N/A	
Francie House	1966	3302	$75.00	
Galleria	1989	4033	N/A	
Glamour Home (furnished)	1985	9477	N/A	
Glamour Home (unfurnished)	1985	9475	N/A	
Hot Dog Stand	1988	4463	N/A	
Hot Rockin' Stage	1986	1144	N/A	
Ice Cream Shoppe	1987	3653	N/A	
Island Fun Hut	1987	4414	N/A	
Jamie's Penthouse	1971	31122	N/A	Sears
Juke Box Music Shop	1988	7361	N/A	
Lively Living House	1970	4961	N/A	
Magical Mansion	1989	4438	N/A	
McDonalds Playset	1994	11774	Rtl	
Mountain Ski Cabin	1972	4283	$35.00	Sears
Movietime Prop Shop	1989	2768	N/A	
New Cafe Today	1970	4983	N/A	
New Restyled Dream House	N/A	4092	$250.00	
Olympic Ski Village	1975	7412	N/A	
Pop-Up Playhouse	1995	13198	Rtl	
Portable House	1962	1428	N/A	Sears
Quick Curl Boutique	1973	8665	N/A	
Record Shop	1989	4030	N/A	
Schoolroom	1965	9343C	$400.00	Sears
Soda Shoppe	1989	2707	N/A	
Sports Shop	1989	4028	N/A	
Step 'n Style Boutique	1989	2769	N/A	
Surprise House	1972	4282	N/A	
Teen Dream Bedroom	1971	4985	N/A	Barbie Place Setting
Three House Group	1967	N/A	N/A	
Three in One House	1995	11418	Rtl	
Town & Country Market	1971	4984	N/A	
Townhouse (furnished)	1984	3764	N/A	
Townhouse (unfurnished)	1980	7825	N/A	
Tropical Pool & Patio	1987	3041	N/A	
Tutti & Chris Patio Picnic House	1967	N/A	N/A	
Tutti & Chris Sleep & Play House	1967	5038	N/A	
Tutti Ice Cream Stand	1967	3563	N/A	

REAL ESTATE

ITEM	YEAR	NUMBER	VALUE	STORE/COLLECTION
Tutti Playhouse, no doll	1967	3300	N/A	
Tutti Playhouse with doll	1967	3306	N/A	
Tutti Summer House	1967	3317	N/A	
Tutti & Todd Playhouse	1966	N/A	N/A	
Tutti & Todd Playhouse without dolls	1966	N/A	N/A	
Wet 'n Wild Lifeguard Stand	1990	3713	N/A	
Wet 'n Wild Water Park	1990	7614	N/A	
World of Barbie Family House	1969	1006	N/A	
World of Barbie House, The	1968	1048	$50.00	

RECORDS

ITEM	YEAR	NUMBER	VALUE
Barbie & Her Friends Record	N/A	N/A	$20.00
Barbie Sings (45 RPM record album)	1961	840	$75.00
Barbie Sings (demo record)	1961	849	$100.00
Busy Barbie	N/A	N/A	$12.00
Here in Nashville Record	1970	N/A	$10.00
Record	1981	N/A	$25.00

Vehicles

Item	Year	Number	Value	Store/Collection
57 Chevy	1989	3561	$75.00	
ATC Cycle	1972	31229	N/A	Sears
Barbie & Ken Dune Buggy	1970	5908	$200.00	
Beach Bus	1974	7805	N/A	
Biking Fun	1994	67053	$8.00	
California Dream Beach Taxi	1988	4520	N/A	
City Nights Cycle	1994	7005	$17.00	
Classy Corvette	1976	9612	N/A	
Convertible	1962	N/A	N/A	
Country Camper	1971	4994	$30.00	
Cruise Ship	1994	10921	$70.00	
Dream Boat	1975	7232	N/A	
Dream Boat Ship	1994	10921	N/A	
Dream 'Vette	1981	3299	N/A	
Ferrari	1988	3136	N/A	
Ferrari 328 GTS	1989	3564	N/A	
Flight Time Airplane	1990	2081	N/A	
Friend Ship	1973	8639	N/A	
Goin' Camping Set with Breeze Buggy	1973	8669	N/A	
Going Boating Set	1973	7738	N/A	
Golden Dream Motorhome	1994	2555	Rtl	
Hot Rod	1963	1460	$200.00	Sears
Hot Rod (red)	1964	1582	N/A	Sears
Jaguar XJS	1994	12386	$20.00	
Mini-Van	1995	13185	$35.00	
Motor Bike	1984	4856	N/A	
Motor Bike	1989	N/A	$5.00	
Motorcycle	1994	419	N/A	
Mustang	1993	65032	$17.00	
Mustang	1995	11929	Rtl	
Orange Roadster	19	N/A	$85.00	
Paint 'n Dazzle Car	1994	10253	$25.00	
Porsche	1994	10876	Rtl	
Sand Buggy	1970	11756	N/A	Montgomery Ward
Silver 'Vette	1984	4934	N/A	
Snowmobile	1972	11796	N/A	Montgomery Ward
Speed Boat	1964	9314	N/A	Sears
Speed Boat	1994	6546	$15.00	Swim 'n Dive
Speed Boat (red)	1972	N/A	N/A	
Splash Cycle	1986	2240	N/A	

VEHICLES

ITEM	YEAR	NUMBER	VALUE	STORE/COLLECTION
Sport Plane	1964	9315C	$2300.00	Sears
Sports Car	1962	1405	$150.00	
Sports Car	1965	1583	N/A	Sears
Sports Car (purple)	1964	1581	N/A	Sears
Sports Cruiser	1995	67163	$10.00	
Star Traveler Motorhome	1980	9794	N/A	
Star 'Vette	1980	9831	N/A	
Starcycle	1978	2149	$20.00	
Starlight Motorhome	1994	11620	$40.00	
Sun 'n Fun Buggy	1971	1158	N/A	
Sunsailor-Catamaran	1976	9106	N/A	
Super Power Motocycle	1995	12538	Rtl	
Super 'Vette (remote control)	1980	1291	N/A	
Ten Speeder	1974	7777	N/A	
Travelin' Trailer	1982	5489	$25.00	
Travelin' Trailer Deluxe Set	1983	5514	N/A	
Ultra 'Vette	1986	2784	N/A	
Volkswagen Cabriolet	1988	3804	N/A	
VW Golf Cabriolet (Hot Wheels)	1988	6803	N/A	
Western Fun Motorhome	1989	3366	N/A	
Western Star Traveler Motorhome	1982	5345	N/A	

5906 40